MARVELOUS
Mercy

MARVELOUS *Mercy*

The Shocking Truth About the Mercy of God

ROBERT E. HENSON

Treasure House
An Imprint of
Destiny Image® Publishers, Inc.
P.O. Box 310
Shippensburg, PA 17257-0310

"For where your treasure is, there will your heart be also."
Matthew 6:21

ISBN 0-7684-2963-3

For Worldwide Distribution
Printed in the U.S.A.

This book and all other Destiny Image, Revival Press, MercyPlace,
Fresh Bread, Destiny Image Fiction, and Treasure House books are available
at Christian bookstores and distributors worldwide.

1 2 3 4 5 6 7 8 9 10 / 09 08 07 06 05 04

For a U.S. bookstore nearest you, call
1-800-722-6774.

For more information on foreign distributors, call
717-532-3040.

Or reach us on the Internet:
www.destinyimage.com

Dedication

This book is offered to honor the Lord Jesus Christ—from whom I have personally received so much mercy.

I also dedicate this volume to each reader—with the prayer that, as a result of reading this book, you will:

- More fully understand the marvelous mercy of the Lord;

- Have greater personal assurance of the application of God's mercy in your life; and,

- Have an increased awe of God's mercy and its efficacy and extended reach.

Robert E. Henson

Acknowledgments

Numerous persons made valuable contributions to this project. Their enthusiastic assistance is noted here with deep and sincere appreciation.

- My wife, Shirley—for her frequent encouragements (and prodding) to write.

- My daughter, Melissa Hudson—for her creative ideas.

- My daughter, Jerusha McGhee—for her enthusiasm about my writing.

- My parents, Rev. Floyd and Ellen Henson—for their prayers for this book.

- My proofreaders, Wanda Fielder (my sister) and Talisa Gauthier (my secretary)—for expert assistance.

- Valerie Crenshaw (my secretary)—for superb help with computerizing my rough drafts.

- Rev. Michael Jewett—for gracious support in research.

- The Staff and Ministers of South Flint Tabernacle, the church I am blessed to serve as Pastor—for serving so capably and faithfully that I have time to write.

- Don Milam, Acquisitions Manager for Destiny Image —for believing in this book.

And to numerous friends—who have frequently offered verbal encouragement for me to keep on writing.

Robert E. Henson

Table of Contents

Foreword

In Exodus 15, we find a song of Moses following the deliverance of the children of Israel. Verse 13 says, "Thou in thy mercy hast led forth the people which thou hast redeemed: thou hast guided them in thy strength unto thy holy habitation."

Mercy led forth the redeemed ones and guided them in strength.

Pastor Robert Henson, with *Marvelous Mercy*, has undertaken a study that will bless and strengthen the reader beyond measure. You cannot contemplate that He is The Father of Mercies—and not find in Him The God of All Comfort.

Just when you think that you've made your last, final, and unforgivable mistake, you hear a whisper from the Psalms that His mercy endureth forever. From beginning to end, Pastor Henson shares his keen insight with this Bible-based study of the unmerited favor of God.

I commend Robert Henson for his outstanding and in-depth study. I commend *Marvelous Mercy* to you the reader—may the book you now hold in your hands bring you truth and hope. If you haven't experienced it yet—or perhaps just need to be reminded—may you learn from these pages the magnificence of God's love for you and the marvelous mercy He extends to you.

T. F. Tenney
Author, *More Power to You.*

CHAPTER ONE

Exploring God's Mercy

Mercy. What an extraordinary and expressive word! Mercy. God's mercy. Only a magnificent Creator could come up with a concept so astonishing as the truth revealed in God's mercy! It is truly one of the most awesome character traits of Almighty God.

Marvelous mercy! Mercy is certainly one of the grandest of all the biblical themes. As a divine gift its beauty has no human comparison. Mercy is absolutely a heavenly object creating marvelous wonder as it is continuously being rediscovered in the hearts and lives of its recipients.

The Greek word for *marvelous* is *thaumaste*. It can also properly be translated as *astonishing*, even *shocking*. The word is most appropriate for describing God's mercy. The mercy of God is absolutely astonishing in its actions toward God's created beings. At times, it is even shocking in the extremes to which it will go to manifest its passion for humankind! It is truly and absolutely marvelous.

The words *mercy* and *grace* are often used interchangeably in religious dialogue. However, scripturally they are two different subjects. These two great doctrines stand as bookends to another very important concept, and that is *justice*. These three have been correctly defined as follows:

Justice—receiving what one deserves

Grace—receiving what one does not deserve

Mercy—not receiving what one deserves

It should be pointed out that for a soul to obtain grace, he or she must first be embraced by mercy. This truth is pointedly made by Jesus Christ himself in perhaps the most quoted verse in the New Testament—John 3:16

> *"For God so loved the world, that he gave his only begotten Son, that whosoever believeth in him should not perish, but have everlasting life."*

It is imperative to notice in the verse above that before God gave, He so loved. In the giving of God, there is the obvious element of *grace* (Greek/*charis*). However, in the matter of *so loving*, there is the equally obvious element of *mercy* (Greek/*eleos*). Let this truth permeate your thinking. *Mercy is the very fountainhead of grace!*

MERCY IS THE VERY FOUNTAINHEAD OF GRACE!

It is told that a mother once approached Napoleon and sought for a pardon for her condemned son. Napoleon retorted that her son deserved to die and did not in any wise deserve mercy. The relentless mother responded that it would not be mercy if her son deserved it, yet mercy was her plea. Napoleon was moved by the mother's earnest appeal and spared the life of her son.

If the wily Napoleon was willing to grant mercy, how much more willing is our Heavenly Father! In fact, a tremendous insight into the nature of our Lord is recorded in Ephesians 2:1-5.

> *"And you hath he quickened, who were dead in trespasses and sins;*
>
> *Wherein in time past ye walked according to the course of this world, according to the prince of the power of the air, the spirit that now worketh in the children of disobedience:*
>
> *Among whom also we all had our conversation in times past in the lusts of our flesh, fulfilling the desires of the flesh and of the mind; and were by nature the children of wrath, even as others.*
>
> *But God, who is rich in mercy, for his great love wherewith he loved us,*
>
> *Even when we were dead in sins, hath quickened us together with Christ, (by grace ye are saved;)"*

Notice again verse 4, "But God, *who is rich in mercy,* for his great love wherewith he loved us." [Emphasis added]

The American Heritage Dictionary defines the word *rich,* as used here, as...*having an abundant supply.*

How unbelievabaly breathtaking! Our God has an abundant supply of *mercy!* It is a fount that will never run dry and a reserve that has no limit.

This insight is reinforced in Romans 10:12 (RSV), which says,

> *"For there is no distinction between Jew and Greek; the same Lord is Lord of all and bestows his riches upon all who call upon him."*

Yet further testimony is found in the Psalms. Pay close attention to these particular verses:

"For thou, Lord, art good, and ready to forgive; and plenteous in mercy unto all them that call upon thee" (Psalm 86:5).

"The LORD is merciful and gracious, slow to anger, and plenteous in mercy" (Psalm 103:8).

The Measure of God's Wealth

God is wealthy. He does not measure His wealth in mutual stocks or corporate bonds. His affluence is measured in the deep reservoirs of *mercy that exist in His eternal nature*. God invests that wealth for the benefit of fallen humanity.

God prefers to measure His vast wealth in terms of mercy, forgiveness, and grace. This is very intriguing, for according to Genesis 14:22 and other scriptures, the Lord is the Most High God—*the Possessor* of the heaven and the earth. God owns it *all*—the whole world and the universe.

Yet God does not strut His material wealth before us. He makes no reference to Wall Street. He does not wow us with statements of financial investments and holdings. He does not boast of the ownership of large corporations.

When Elvis Presley was alive, he owned numerous large diamonds, rare gems, and other exquisite pieces of jewelry. It has been told that he would sometimes bring them out and dazzle his close friends with them.

But God is not into bangles or baubles or beads. When God wants to impress us with His vast wealth, He can simply pull back the curtain of time and space and unveil the richness of His marvelous mercy as manifested in His incredible willingness to forgive our sins and also by the granting of His amazing grace!

This idea is also exemplified in the wonderful biblical act of redemption. The Greek word for *redemption* is *agorazo*. It conveys the notion of one entering a slave market and spending his money to purchase a slave for the express purpose of setting him or her free. God gets great pleasure in lavishing His mercy on undeserving, yet repentant, souls.

Consider this testimony from Romans 11:33:

> "O the depth of the riches both of the wisdom and knowledge of God! How unsearchable are his judgments, and his ways past finding out!"

Observe the phrase *the depth of the riches...of God*. The connotation is that God has *deep pockets*. He can give and keep on giving. He can give extravagantly and never run out of supply.

Here is another scriptural witness, found in Ephesians 3:8.

> "Unto me, who am less than the least of all saints, is this grace given, that I should preach among the Gentiles the unsearchable riches of Christ."

Reflect on the expression *the unsearchable riches of Christ*. This means that He is so wealthy that we will never discover all of His riches. They are beyond our ability to even calculate or comprehend.

Let us view yet another biblical witness in Romans 2:4.

> "Or despisest thou the riches of his goodness and forbearance and longsuffering; not knowing that the goodness of God leadeth thee to repentance?"

In this verse we are informed of three aspects of God's wealth:

- He is rich in *goodness* = His excellence in character
- He is rich in *forbearance* = His self-restraint and tolerance in putting up with "jerks"
- He is rich in *longsuffering* = His patience in waiting for persons to come to repentance

Vessels of Mercy

Romans 9:22-24 says:

> *"What if God, willing to shew his wrath, and to make his power known, endured with much longsuffering the **vessels of wrath** fitted to destruction:*
>
> *And that he might make known the riches of his glory on the **vessels of mercy**, which he had afore prepared unto glory,*
>
> *Even us, whom he hath called, not of the Jews only, but also of the Gentiles?" [Emphasis added]*

These are unique and meaningful verses of scripture. Verse 22 informs us that God has, for a prolonged time, put up with *vessels of wrath*, which are persons deserving of and headed to destruction.

Verse 23 tells us why God is patient when judgment is, in fact, so long overdue—*that He might make known the riches of His glory to the vessels of mercy.* These vessels of mercy are the people the Lord has called unto salvation and eternal glory.

A *vessel*, according to *The American Heritage Dictionary*, is *a container; a person seen as the agent or embodiment, as of a quality: a vessel of mercy.* Wow!

Thus it is that some folks are containers into which *wrath* will be poured. Others are repentant, and, therefore, containers into which God will pour His *mercy*. A good question to ask is, "Which kind of a vessel am I?"

Romans 2:4-11 illustrates this truth:

> *"Or despisest thou the riches of his goodness and forbearance and longsuffering; not knowing that the goodness of God leadeth thee to repentance?*
>
> *But after thy hardness and impenitent heart treasurest up unto thyself wrath against the day of wrath and revelation of the righteous judgment of God;*
>
> *Who will render to every man according to his deeds:*

To them who by patient continuance in well doing seek for glory and honour and immortality, eternal life:

But unto them that are contentious, and do not obey the truth, but obey unrighteousness, indignation and wrath,

Tribulation and anguish, upon every soul of man that doeth evil, of the Jew first, and also of the Gentile;

But glory, honour, and peace, to every man that worketh good, to the Jew first, and also to the Gentile:

For there is no respect of persons with God."

Have Mercy on Me

The psalmist whispered this plea to the Almighty in Psalm 33:22:

"Let thy mercy, O LORD, be upon us, according as we hope in thee."

It was blind Bartimaeus who halted the travel of Christ with the earnest prayer recorded in Mark 10:47:

"Jesus, thou son of David, have mercy on me."

At least five other times in the ministry of Christ, persons approached Jesus with this urgent appeal, "Have mercy on me!" It is noteworthy that *Jesus never rejected such a plea!*

Ingredients of Mercy

The word mercy appears 276 times in some 261 verses of the King James Version of the Bible. According to the estimate of Jesus Christ, mercy is one of the weightiest—or most important—matters in life. His statement with regard to this is given in Matthew 23:23 (TLB):

*"Yes, woe upon you, Pharisees, and you other religious leaders-hypocrites! For you tithe down to the last mint leaf in your garden, but ignore the **important thing—justice and mercy and faith.** Yes, you should tithe,*

but you shouldn't leave the more important things
undone." [Emphasis added]

Mercy is a composite of several sterling virtues. Consider this
teaching of our Lord as recorded in Luke 6:36-37 (NASU):

"Be merciful, just as your Father is merciful.

*Do not judge, and you will not be judged; and do not
condemn, and you will not be condemned; pardon, and
you will be pardoned."*

From these two brief scriptures we learn the following traits of
mercy:

- Mercy is *not judgmental;*
- Mercy is *non-condemning;* and,
- Mercy *grants release or pardon.*

The parabolic teaching of Jesus in Matthew 18:26-27 (NAS) adds
to the list of known ingredients in mercy.

*"The slave therefore falling down, prostrated himself
before him, saying, 'Have patience with me, and I will
repay you everything.'*

*And the lord of that slave felt compassion and released
him and forgave him the debt."*

Here we discover these additional elements of mercy:

- Mercy exercises *patience;*
- Mercy manifests *compassion, or love in action;* and,
- Mercy *forgives.*

A related word in the Scriptures is *atonement.* The Hebrew
word for *atonement* is *kaphar.* It conveys the following notions:

- *To cover over (as to overlook);*
- *To expiate or make atonement for a fault or an offense;*
- *To pardon;*
- *To reconcile; and,*
- *To treat as forgiven.*

One of the Hebrew words for *forgive* is *nasa*. It expresses the following nuances of ideas:

- *To lift up;*
- *To hold up (as in sustain);*
- *To accept;*
- *To carry;*
- *To forgive sin;*
- *To bear in the stead of another; and,*
- *To help.*

The word *nasa* has many shades of meaning, but the concept of *lifting up* (in some form) strongly permeates most of them. It should not go unnoticed that the arm of the United States Government which lifts people into space, the National Aeronautics and Space Administration, has for its acronym, NASA.

One of the Hebrew words for *mercy* is *checed*. It denotes the following:

- *To feel and respond with kindness;*
- *To be merciful; and,*
- *To love steadfastly.*

Another of the Hebrew words translated *mercy* is *chanan*. It connotes the following:

- *To bend or stoop in kindness to an inferior;*
- *To bestow favor; and,*
- *To grant mercy.*

Yet another word in the Hebrew for *mercy* is *racham*. It conveys the following ideas:

- *To give tender affection;*
- *To care deeply;*
- *To love;*
- *To soothe; and,*
- *To have compassion upon.*

Mercy conveys the notion of caressing as a mother does a baby, or to bear up gently as one would pick up an injured child. Such is the marvelous mercy of God to us.

MERCY IS THE READINESS OF GOD TO ACT NOW.

The Greek word for *mercy* is *eleos*. According to *Vine's Expository Dictionary of Old and New Testament Words, eleos* "is the outward manifestation of pity; it assumes need on the part of him who receives it, and resources adequate to meet the need on the part of him who shows it."

E. W. Bullinger, in *A Critical Lexicon and Concordance to the English and Greek New Testament*, defines *eleos* as "a feeling of sympathy with misery, active compassion, the desire of relieving the miserable."

Dr. Joseph Thayer adds more flavor to the definition of eleos (mercy) in *A Greek-English Lexicon of the New Testament*. There he espouses that it includes "readiness to help those in trouble."

Mercy is that attribute of perfection whereby God pities and relieves the miseries of humanity. Someone has said that *mercy is the readiness of God to act now*. I really like that. That expresses the intrinsic nature of God's mercy.

Vessels of Mercy on Display

1 Timothy 1:15-17 states:

> *"This is a faithful saying, and worthy of all acceptation, that Christ Jesus came into the world to save sinners; of whom I am chief.*
>
> *Howbeit for this cause I obtained mercy, that in me first Jesus Christ might shew forth all longsuffering, for a pattern to them which should hereafter believe on him to life everlasting.*
>
> *Now unto the King eternal, immortal, invisible, the only wise God, be honour and glory for ever and ever. Amen."*

Christ Jesus came to save *sinners*. Paul confessed to being the worst of sinners. Paul declares that God saved him specifically for the purpose of using him as a pattern, as an example or illustration of just how far God's mercy could reach. Paul was a *trophy* of God's mercy!

How about you and me? Here's what Ephesians 2:7 has to say:

> *"That* **in the ages to come he might shew the exceeding riches of his grace in his kindness toward** *us through Christ Jesus."* *[Emphasis added]*

The fact is that God will put His Church on display in eternity. The Lord will proclaim to the angels and to all the heavenly hosts, "Look! This is what My mercy and grace did! I saved persons who appeared hopeless."

And the redeemed will sing, "Your grace and mercy brought me through…"

To whom is such wealth and riches of mercy available?

Romans 10:11-14 answers that question:

> *"For the scripture saith, Whosoever believeth on him shall not be ashamed.*
>
> *For there is no difference between the Jew and the Greek: for the same Lord over all is rich unto all that call upon him.*
>
> *For whosoever shall call upon the name of the Lord shall be saved.*
>
> *How then shall they call on him in whom they have not believed? and how shall they believe in him of whom they have not heard? and how shall they hear without a preacher?"*

The wealth and riches of mercy are available to all who call upon the name of the Lord. Thank God for preachers who declare the whole counsel of God. If you have such a preacher in your life, you are blessed. If you don't have such a preacher, ask God to lead you to one.

The scholarly entomologist, Henri Fabre, expressed this conclusion with reference to the insect known as the gnat. He said, "Human knowledge will be erased from the archives of the world before we possess the last word about even a gnat."

That being true about the gnat, how much more is that conclusion applicable to the marvelous mercy of God! On this earth we will never fully comprehend God's marvelous mercy. It will continue to remain a mystery. It will persist in shocking us with its scandalous actions.

However, in the succeeding chapters, we will attempt to at least expand your understanding of the awesomeness of the mercy of Almighty God. It will be worth our while to uncover some of the rare gems that will help us to have a better appreciation for the Father's marvelous mercy.

CHAPTER TWO

The Father Of Mercies

2 Corinthians 1:3 says:

> *"Blessed be God, even the Father of our Lord Jesus Christ, the Father of mercies, and the God of all comfort."*

The Bible reveals some 700 titles belonging to God. If the indirect inferences are included, the total exceeds 1,300 titles. Each of the titles of God has significance. They usually indicate something of God's character or nature and/or some relationship He has with mankind.

In 2 Corinthians 1:3, the Apostle Paul uses one of those titles. It is a title that is pregnant with meaning. Paul refers to the Almighty God as *the Father of mercies*. There is much more to this title of God than we first realize when we read it. Let us give this title a closer examination.

The Significance of Father

According to *The American Heritage Dictionary*, *father*, as used here, means *"A man who creates, originates, or founds something: Chaucer is considered the father of English poetry."*

It could also be said that Aristotle is the father of the modern library and that Noah Webster is the father of the modern dictionary.

From this definition we get our first clue about this title of God. He is the Creator and Originator of mercy! In other words, mercy is not a commodity that God acquired somewhere in time.

God is, quite literally, the Big Daddy of mercy!

MERCY HAS THE DNA OF THE EVERLASTING FATHER

When any inquiring soul takes the time to study the genes of this awesome gift called *mercy*, he or she will always discover that *mercy has the DNA of the Everlasting Father.*

God is the Begetter, the Father, and the Original Giver of all mercies!

The Father of Mercies

Mercies is the plural form of the word mercy. In other words, God is not just the *Father* of the concept or the gift called mercy, but He is the *Initiator* of the actual practice of extending mercy!

Furthermore, God grants mercy not just once, but He gives mercy in multiple donations! Where would you and I be were it not for the Father of mercies?

Jeremiah stated it like this in Lamentations 3:22-23:

> *"It is of the LORD's mercies that we are not consumed, because his compassions fail not.*
>
> *They are new every morning: great is thy faithfulness."*

This truth should grab your heart and elicit from you and me a holy "Wow!" Our only hope for eternal salvation is tied to the fact that The Almighty God is also the Father of mercies. His faithfulness is beyond our comprehension. His compassions fail not. His mercies are fresh every morning.

Obtaining Mercy

The Word of God declares the need for each person to experience cleansing from sin. The Holy Bible also reveals that such forgiveness for sin is available through the Lord Jesus Christ, our Savior.

Note 1 Corinthians 6:9-11:

> *"Know ye not that the unrighteous shall not inherit the kingdom of God? Be not deceived: neither fornicators, nor idolaters, nor adulterers, nor effeminate, nor abusers of themselves with mankind,*
>
> *Nor thieves, nor covetous, nor drunkards, nor revilers, nor extortioners, shall inherit the kingdom of God.*
>
> *And such were some of you: but ye are washed, but ye are sanctified, but ye are justified in **the name of the Lord Jesus,** and by **the Spirit of our God.**"*
> [Emphasis added]

Notice the life changes mentioned above.

- Washed
- Sanctified
- Justified

How was all this accomplished? What were the Divine tools?

- The Name of the Lord Jesus
- The Holy Spirit

Our God is the Father of mercies!

An Apparent Dilemma

In Luke 18:9-14, we read:

> *"And he spake this parable unto certain which trusted in themselves that they were righteous, and despised others:*
>
> *Two men went up into the temple to pray; the one a Pharisee, and the other a publican.*

The Pharisee stood and prayed thus with himself, God, I thank thee, that I am not as other men are, extortioners, unjust, adulterers, or even as this publican.

I fast twice in the week, I give tithes of all that I possess.

And the publican, standing afar off, would not lift up so much as his eyes unto heaven, but smote upon his breast, saying, God be merciful to me a sinner.

I tell you, this man went down to his house justified rather than the other: for every one that exalteth himself shall be abased; and he that humbleth himself shall be exalted."

The word *dilemma*, according to *The American Heritage Dictionary*, means a *predicament that seemingly defies a satisfactory solution.*

The reality is that there is no such thing as a dilemma for God. God is never in a state of quandary or panic as to what should be done. However, in the masterful story that Jesus related in the above scriptures, Jesus himself presents for our consideration an apparent dilemma for the Father of mercies.

Here are the horns of the problem:

- Does God prefer, bless, and accept someone whose actions are proper but whose attitude is so arrogant and proud that it stinks?
- Or, does He prefer, bless, and accept someone whose decorum is sometimes deficient but who is humble and given to repentance?

Does God have a preference?

Before we go any further, it should be expressed here and now that a good attitude is no license for sin. However, this illustrative and instructional story, told from the lips of Jesus, leaves us in no doubt as to the divine summation and resolution of this apparent dilemma.

Let us take a closer look at some of the pertinent and contrasting details of this parable.

The Pharisee

The Pharisee was a member of an ultra-conservative religious order. As a matter of fact, the Pharisees were extremely rigorous and stringent about even the minute details of code and conduct.

No doubt, there were some sincere Pharisees. As a religious movement, though, the Pharisees, and particularly their leaders, had lost the heart of true devotion and were hung up on ceremonialism and pontification.

In this story of Jesus', the Pharisee belonged with the majority of the religious order who had become world-class hypocrites. For instance, this Pharisee was a *liar*. How do we

THE STARTLING TRUTH IS THAT THE PUBLICAN WAS MORE ACCEPTABLE IN THE SIGHT OF GOD THAN THE PHARISEE!

know that? His own speech is testimony against him. Capture the distilled essence of dishonesty as he utters, "I am not as other men are." By this expression he exempts himself from the depravity of humanity. Romans 3:23 (ASV) shows the fallacy of the Pharisee's estimation of himself:

"for all have sinned, and fall short of the glory of God."

Furthermore, this Pharisee was suffering from *personal deception*. He bragged, "I am not...as [like] this publican." He was confident that he was better than the publican. However, *the startling truth is that the publican was more acceptable in the sight of God than the Pharisee!*

The Publican

In contrast to the Pharisee, the publican was a tax-gatherer for the Roman government. Publicans were generally known as con artists, liars, and cheats. Sometimes they were abusive, manipulative, and even vengeful.

This publican, however, knew some important truths and acted upon them. He knew there was a God, so he went to His House and prayed to Him. This publican also knew that he himself was a sinner. He even called himself one! The publican knew that he was guilty, so he felt condemned and ashamed. He would not so much as lift his eyes to heaven.

The publican also knew some other facts and principles. He knew what he needed—he needed mercy. He was also aware of how to receive mercy. He confessed his personal depravity and called upon the Father of mercies to supply his need for pardon.

A Few More Comparisons

Let us briefly observe some other contrasts between these two men who went into the Temple to pray.

The Pharisee was:

- Self-righteous—he trusted in self;
- Insensitive—he had no sense of personal transgression;
- Arrogant—he was lacking in humility; and,
- Hardened—he felt no compelling need for God.

The result of the Pharisee's Temple attendance and prayer was that he went home without God's acceptance or approval on his life. God was not pleased with the Pharisee. *His sins went home with him!*

The publican was:

- Sincere—he exhibited no fakery or hypocrisy;
- Transparent—his prayer was honest: (this counts much with God); and,
- Humble—he asked for what he needed.

The result of the publican's Temple attendance and prayer was that he went home *justified* by the Father of mercies. The publican went home *forgiven*. Additionally, I believe that he went home *happy*. Whenever the load of sin is lifted off of someone's heart, it always follows that they feel greatly relieved and even joyful.

The Rest of The Story

This introduction of the Pharisee and the publican story establishes the fact that Jesus had two types of people in mind when He gave this illustration. First, were those who are *self-righteous*. Such individuals don't feel any consuming need for a Savior. If you will, they consider themselves their own savior.

Second, Jesus directed this parable to those who are *judgmental*. Such folks look on others with contempt and disdain. These folks tend to appoint themselves as the judge for all their fellow human beings.

Jesus himself gave the interpretation of the parable—what we often call the moral of the story.

> *"for every one that exalteth himself shall be abased; and he that humbleth himself shall be exalted"* (Luke 18:14b).

Here again are the traits of those who practice self-exaltation:

- Trust in self
- No real need for a Savior
- Judgmental toward fellow human beings

The results of self-exaltation are that such persons will be *abased*, meaning they will:

- Be reduced in God's view to the true level of his or her unworthiness (in other words, God isn't impressed) and
- Forfeit the mercy they could have received.

The contrast highlighted by Christ is found in those who *humble themselves*. The traits these people showcase are:

- Honesty and transparency with God regarding the true state of their spiritual life;
- Meaningful repentance; and,
- Tolerance toward the rest of humanity.

The Lord Jesus concluded that such humble persons shall be *exalted*. In light of the emphasis given in the parable, we can rightly assume that the meaning of exaltation in this regard includes these blessings:

- Being forgiven!

- Being justified!

- Being lifted in spirit!

Oh, the miracle of *Divine acceptance*! It is because of the Father of mercies that you and I can obtain forgiveness and salvation. No wonder Fanny Crosby, the blind, prolific songwriter of yesteryear, wrote the following lines of earnest plea:

> "Pass me not, O gentle Savior,
> Hear my humble cry;
> While on others Thou art calling,
> Do not pass me by.
>
> Let me at Thy throne of mercy
> Find a sweet relief,
> Kneeling there in deep contrition;
> Help my unbelief.
>
> Savior, Savior,
> Hear my humble cry;
> While on others Thou art calling,
> Do not pass me by.

Jesus is just waiting for you to cry out to Him. He loves to forgive. O, marvelous mercy!

CHAPTER THREE

The House of Mercy

John 5:2 says:

> *"Now there is at Jerusalem by the sheep market a pool, which is called in the Hebrew tongue Bethesda, having five porches."*

The ruins of the pool named Bethesda still remain to this day and can be seen when one visits Jerusalem. The word *Bethesda* means *house of mercy*.

Mercy is one of the most beautiful of all spiritual actions of God on behalf of man. Mercy is more inspiring than Niagara Falls. We can be mesmerized by the majestic flow of water over the Niagara cliffs, but we will never behold anything in life that is more beautiful than mercy. I shall

MERCY IS ONE OF GOD'S ALL-TIME GREATEST MASTERPIECES.

never forget the day I was flying in a commercial airliner and looked out the window, beholding the majestic snow-covered peaks of the Alps below. It was so awe-inspiring to know that mercy is as breathtaking spiritually as the majestic Alps are naturally.

Mercy is one of heaven's classics and one of the great wonders from the heavenly realms. Mercy is one of God's all-time greatest masterpieces. There's one entire chapter in the Bible that is devoted to recognition and exaltation of God for His mercy. It is Psalm 136. The last phrase of each verse in the chapter is *for His mercy endureth forever*. Here are just two of the many reasons for praising God that are given to us in this celebrated chapter:

- He remembered us in our low estate.
- He redeemed us from our enemies.

Yes, each of us has a testimony recollecting how the Father rescued us from our enemies!

The mercy of God will never be fully fathomed by the human mind. God's mercy defies explanation and reaches beyond our ability to comprehend it.

The number one ingredient of mercy is the *goodness of God*. This is essentially conveyed in Psalm 136:1, which says,

> *"O give thanks unto the LORD; for he is good: for his mercy endureth for ever."*

Because of God's innate goodness:

- We have not been consumed;
- We have been led to repent;
- We have been forgiven; and,
- We have the promise of heaven.

Human Response Required

Some feel that mercy is all up to God and that we have absolutely no part to play in it. That is incorrect. There are some responsibilities placed upon us if we would receive the mercy appropriated from God. These requirements include:

- Humbling ourselves;
- Repenting;
- Asking God for His mercy; and,
- Forgiving others of their offenses against us.

These are the attitudes that attract the mercy of God. With reference to forgiving others—if they don't make it right, they'll still have to answer for it. However, when you forgive them, you take it out of your hands, and you put it squarely into the hands of God. This is an imperative necessity because ill will and an unforgiving spirit will zap every aspect of your spiritual life!

King David

Prior to the Prophet Nathan coming to King David to reprove him, David was guilty of several sins:

- Lust;
- Adultery;
- Murder; and,
- Attempted cover-up.

David had a choice to make when confronted with his sins. He could have reacted angrily. He could have even had the prophet executed on the spot. Instead, traditional history says that David stepped down off the throne and removed his crown. He then flung himself to the ground and began to weep and repent from deep within his soul. Psalm 51 records his prayer of contrition.

Two of King David's sins were capital offenses, namely, murder and adultery. The law called for execution of the guilty. There was no provision in the Mosaic Law for atonement for either of these types of transgressions. Observe the lament of King David recorded in Psalm 51:16:

"For thou desirest not sacrifice; else would I give it: thou delightest not in burnt offering."

David apparently inquired what sacrifices a guilty person could make to atone for adultery and murder. He was informed that there were not any.

When there was no acceptable and efficacious sacrifice available, King David took the only hopeful action left—he pleaded for God's mercy. When there wasn't any provision in the law, and when

35

there was no means of atonement, David pleaded with God for mercy. And the prophet declared in 2 Samuel 12:13 (NIV),

> *"The LORD has taken away your sin. You are not going to die."*

Human Imperfections

The devil sometimes hammers people, forcing them to think that God is going to cut them off because of their imperfections. Please note that my reference here regards imperfections, not hypocrisy. There is a vast difference between the two. Hypocrisy involves insincerity. God will not overlook that.

There are times in each Christian's life when, though we reach for the top rung of the ladder of consecration and devotion, we come short of the mark. The devil enjoys coming alongside of us at such times. He volunteers to review our spiritual report card with us. He relishes rubbing our deficiencies and failures in our face. However, there is *mercy* in the House of Mercy.

Sometimes a low grade on a test causes us to have to take the test again. Thankfully, though, God is there to welcome us back. Mercy, mercy, mercy, mercy, mercy, mercy!

Don't ever forget that it was Jesus who taught us to forgive our brother or sister no less than 490 times, even for the same offense, and even within the same day. Somebody made the observation that if you really forgive, you don't keep track of the number of times you have granted forgiveness.

We've all come short of the glory of God, but I don't remember committing a foul 490 times in one day, especially the same foul. Friend, if God requires you and I to forgive so freely and copiously, rest assured that He will do the same and much more!

AS YOU AND I KEEP ASKING FOR MERCY, GOD'S GOING TO KEEP GIVING IT.

The devil sometimes suggests to believers to quit asking for mercy. Do you know why? It is because he knows that as long as you and I keep asking for mercy, God's going to keep giving it.

Queen Esther

Israel was in jeopardy. The agreement reached between Queen Esther and Mordecai was that after three days of fasting and prayer, Esther would make a direct appeal to King Ahasuerus to spare the Jews.

The law of the Persian and Mede Empire was that anyone entering the throne room of the king uninvited was subject to being summarily executed. The only action that could save such a person from sure death was the king holding out to them the golden royal scepter.

After the three days of seeking God, Esther dressed herself in her finest. She made her way to the throne room. No doubt she took a deep breath before stepping through the doors to approach the king.

Tradition gives us some additional information. It tells us that when Esther went in, she was so faint from her three days of fasting and from fear, that when she got in front of the king, she actually collapsed into the arms of the servant. She swooned. King Ahasuerus looked at her and was astonished! He immediately extended the golden scepter.

Perhaps King Ahasuerus could see the fear written all over her face. It is believed that the king then inquired as to her fear and her fainting. Esther informed him that it was out of her concern over the law relative to approaching the king without invitation.

It was then that the king informed Esther that she had no reason to be afraid. He declared that the law applied to everyone in the kingdom except the wife of the king. She was always welcome in the throne room of the king. For her, the throne room was a perpetual house of mercy!

That is precisely how God wants us to feel about His Throne Room.

Hebrews 4:16 says,

> *"Let us therefore come boldly unto the throne of grace, that we may obtain mercy, and find grace to help in time of need."*

Did you get it? There is both *grace* and *mercy* in His Throne Room and House of Mercy. Because of that, you can make it!

CHAPTER FOUR

The Mercy Seat

Exodus 25:9-11; 16-22 states:

> "According to all that I shew thee, after the pattern of the tabernacle, and the pattern of all the instruments thereof, even so shall ye make it.
>
> And they shall make an ark of shittim wood: two cubits and a half shall be the length thereof, and a cubit and a half the breadth thereof, and a cubit and a half the height thereof.
>
> And thou shalt overlay it with pure gold, within and without shalt thou overlay it, and shalt make upon it a crown of gold round about."
>
> "And thou shalt put into the ark the testimony which I shall give thee.
>
> And thou shalt make a mercy seat of pure gold: two cubits and a half shall be the length thereof, and a cubit and a half the breadth thereof.
>
> And thou shalt make two cherubims of gold, of beaten work shalt thou make them, in the two ends of the mercy seat.

And make one cherub on the one end, and the other cherub on the other end: even of the mercy seat shall ye make the cherubims on the two ends thereof.

And the cherubims shall stretch forth their wings on high, covering the mercy seat with their wings, and their faces shall look one to another; toward the mercy seat shall the faces of the cherubims be.

And thou shalt put the mercy seat above upon the ark; and in the ark thou shalt put the testimony that I shall give thee.

And there I will meet with thee, and I will commune with thee from above the mercy seat, from between the two cherubims which are upon the ark of the testimony, of all things which I will give thee in commandment unto the children of Israel."

The most fascinating piece of furniture in the Old Testament house of worship, which was called the Tabernacle, was the Ark of the Covenant. It was a unit of considerable complexity. The basic box itself was not imposing in size. It measured 45-60 inches in length, 27-36 inches in width, and its height was also 27-36 inches. However, due to the extensive use of gold, the Ark of the Covenant was apparently quite heavy.

The basic storage area was made of acacia or shittim wood and was overlaid within and without with pure gold. In addition to the basic box, there was an ornate crown molding, also made of gold.

There were also two cherubims attached to the lid of the Ark and hovering over it. Each of these cherubims was a solid piece of beaten gold.

The lid of the Ark was called the Mercy Seat. It was also made of pure gold. All of this gold, along with the contents of the Ark, accounted for its weight. Some have estimated that the Ark of the Covenant weighed upwards of 1,000 pounds—half a ton.

The Ark of the Covenant was the symbol in Israel of the presence of Almighty God. The Ark of the Covenant was transported by two staves or poles that were attached one on each side. It was carried on the shoulders of four priests. If, indeed, it weighed one-half ton, each priest was carrying about 250 pounds.

The point we should notice and acknowledge is that being responsible for the transporting of the presence of God was no casual job. The priests assigned to this duty carried a treasure of considerable weight. This ministry was not a light matter. It should also be stated that no ministry should ever be undertaken with a flippant or casual attitude.

An interesting detail, floated down through Jewish oral tradition, is that, though the Ark was quite heavy, the priests who transported it actually felt no weight at all. If that is true, the mercy of God manifested at the Mercy Seat actually made their burden weightless. Is that not indeed what God's mercy does in our lives?

All of this detail leads us to focus on the most significant part of the Ark of the Covenant. That was, without question, the Mercy Seat. Let's examine it more closely.

Its Name and Purpose

First of all, I am fascinated by its given name. The Lord gave this part of the Ark its name. It was named after one of God's most significant attributes or character traits—*mercy*. It was called *the Mercy Seat*.

Stop and think with me—Why did God choose this name over some of the other of His outstanding attributes? Not only is God Merciful, He is also: Wisdom, Omniscient, Omnipotent, Truth, Creator, Giver of Joy, Love, Source of Peace, and Holy.

Why was this seat not named…

- The Wisdom Seat?
- The Knowledge Seat?

- The Power Seat?
- The Truth Seat?
- The Creation Seat?
- The Grace Seat?
- The Happy Seat?
- The Love Seat?
- The Peace Seat?
- The Holy Seat?

The reason the Mercy Seat was so named is that this seat was the precise place where humanity would *meet with* and *commune with* the Almighty God.

Think of it! Man, sin-stained and imperfect, permitted to *meet with* a flawless and thoroughly Holy God!

Consider it! Man, a mere mortal, allowed and enabled to *commune with* The Eternal One!

Intrinsically and ultimately, only God's Mercy could ever bring about such a meeting and provide such communication and fellowship. Were this seat called…

- The Wisdom Seat—you and I could never relate to God on such a superior level.
- The Knowledge Seat—we would never be smart enough to parley with God.
- The Power Seat—humanity is far too weak to interact with God on such a basis.
- The Truth Seat—you and I have had far too much falsehood in our lives to survive an encounter with unyielding and exacting truth.
- The Creation Seat—this is a dimension of ability far beyond human powers.
- The Grace Seat—to get to grace, a person must pass by and be embraced by mercy first.
- The Happy Seat—eternal joy is not possible for sinful flesh.

- The Peace Seat—there is no peace, saith my God, unto the wicked.
- The Love Seat—we had to become friends of God first before we could become lovers of God.
- The Holiness Seat—you and I would not have had any hope of ever knowing God on such a lofty and pure level.

Oh, thank God for mercy! All praises to God that there is a Mercy Seat!

Mercy is the Address
Where a *Relationship* with God Begins

Mercy allows us to:

- *Meet with* God;
- *Communicate with* God;
- Receive *forgiveness* for our sins;
- *Come to know* God; and,
- *Fellowship with* God.

Without God's abundant and everlasting mercy, not one of us would have a ghost of a chance of being saved. Mercy is the *address* where a relationship with God begins.

The View from Above

The Ark of the Covenant was a container and vault for some very precious cargo. However, it was not just a portable museum. It was a laboratory—preserving evidence that would have been acceptable in a court of law.

The evidence contained in the Ark of the Covenant would serve as a witness against Israel should they depart from the one true God. Tablets of stone recorded God's Word; Aaron's budding rod proved God's miracles; and, the golden pot of manna provided proof of God's provisions. Each of these things was evidence of what the eternal God had done for Israel.

The Mercy Seat was made of *pure* gold. Some theologians believe the gold was so pure that it was transparent. In other words, as God looked down upon the Mercy Seat, He could see right through it. God certainly had that ability whether or not the gold was transparent. He could look right through the Mercy Seat and into the interior of the Ark of the Covenant and behold the evidence against a sinful people. This brings us to the Day of Atonement and the application of the blood. It is key for us to understand that *blood is the one thing God has refused to see through!*

When the blood was applied to the Mercy Seat, it covered the evidence! All of the evidence of your sin and my sin is covered by the blood. There is no law that can convict because the evidence has been removed by the blood of Jesus. That ought to produce a glorious shout of thanksgiving.

The New Testament Mercy Seat

The Mercy Seat of the Old Testament has been replaced with something even better in the New Testament—a Person. That's right. The piece of furniture has been replaced with something infinitely superior—a living, communicating, and compassionate Person.

Romans 3:23-25 says:

> *"For all have sinned, and come short of the glory of God;*
>
> *Being justified freely by his grace through the redemption that is in Christ Jesus:*
>
> *Whom God hath set forth to be a propitiation through faith in his blood, to declare his righteousness for the remission of sins that are past, through the forbearance of God."*

Verse 25 speaks of Christ becoming our propitiation. The Greek word for *propitiation* is *hilasterion*. It can also properly be translated mercy seat. In the New Testament, now, and for all time, Jesus Christ is our Mercy Seat. It is in Him that we find and receive full pardon.

The means of our coming to this mercy is through the gospel of The Lord Jesus Christ! That gospel is clearly given to us in Acts 2:38 and numerous other New Testament scriptures.

THE BLOOD OF JESUS DOESN'T JUST COVER THE EVIDENCE OF OUR WRONGDOING AND SINS; IT REMOVES THE EVIDENCE!

And think of this awesome truth—The blood of Jesus doesn't just cover the evidence of our wrongdoing and sins; it *removes* the evidence!

Oh, what a Savior!! Marvelous mercy!

CHAPTER FIVE

The Day Mercy Became Available 24/7

Mark 15:37-39 says:

"And Jesus cried with a loud voice, and gave up the ghost.

And the veil of the temple was rent in twain from the top to the bottom.

And when the centurion, which stood over against him, saw that he so cried out, and gave up the ghost, he said, Truly this man was the Son of God."

The term 24/7 is one that has come into prominent use in the last decade. It is used primarily with reference to businesses that never close. The designation 24/7 indicates that the store is always open and that the services are continually available.

MERCY, AS WE KNOW IT, WAS NOT ALWAYS AVAILABLE 24/7

Mercy, as we know it, was not always available 24/7. The Old Testament pointedly stipulates that the Day of Atonement came only once each year. On that special day, and only on that day, the High Priest would enter beyond the sacred veil and into the Holy of Holies of the Tabernacle or Temple. There, the High Priest would offer blood to make atonement for the sins of the people—sins that had accumulated over the last year.

Please note this carefully—there was no such thing back then as just slipping into the Holy of Holies on an ordinary day to seek atonement and pardon. Nor did a person resort there in the middle of the night because he or she felt compunction to pray and seek God's mercy. In fact, the common person could *never* enter there. The average citizen, or even the elite, could not make his or her personal appeal at the Mercy Seat. The Holy of Holies was accessible only to one man, the High Priest, and even to him *it was only open for business one day out of each year!*

The Crucifixion Of Jesus

Each of the four New Testament gospel writers gives us vivid accounts and important details about the trial and crucifixion of Jesus. Three of the four include a most fascinating and significant reference to the veil of the Temple.

The Temple was located some 600 yards—more than a quarter of a mile—from the place of the execution of Jesus. Yet, coinciding precisely with the time of the expiration of Jesus, the veil in the Temple was miraculously rent in two.

This was a deliberate tearing. So much so that a witness or witnesses saw it happen and watched in awe as it came apart. The Scriptures dutifully note that the tearing of this thick and sacred fabric occurred from the top to the bottom, thus indicating it was an action from heaven.

According to Jewish authorities, the veil was made of strong fabric and was tightly woven. It was at least four inches thick. It was checked yearly to be sure it had not deteriorated in any way. It has been stated that a pair of oxen hooked to each end of the veil could not have ripped it in two.

A casual observer may think this event interesting and move on without further inquiry, but not so with those who understand the significance of that veil. That veil had been a divine barricade to keep out the masses of humanity. Mercy, in a certain sense, had been imprisoned behind that divinely instituted wall.

But now the barricade was down! The gate was open! In fact, the gate was left open! Entrance and access for all persons desiring God's pardon was opened up and made available.

It should also be noted that the veil was rent "in the midst" or in the middle. This was no side entrance. The veil was opened immediately in front of the Mercy Seat. Direct access was thereby granted to God's mercy.

The day that Jesus died is *the day mercy became available 24/7!*

What 24/7 Mercy Means to You and Me

The split veil extends to us an open door for *repentance*. We can repent *anywhere* and at *any time* of the day or night. What a privilege, and what an opportunity!

It means that we can come as *often* as necessary. We can receive as *much* mercy as we need, for the supply is inexhaustible.

It indicates that God's mercy is fully efficacious to meet our deepest need of forgiveness. Oh, how appreciative and thankful we all should be for *the day mercy became available 24/7!*

The Price Jesus Paid to Offer Us Peace

In Isaiah 53:4-5, we read:

> *"Surely he hath borne our griefs, and carried our sorrows: yet we did esteem him stricken, smitten of God, and afflicted.*

49

But he was wounded for our transgressions, he was
bruised for our iniquities: the chastisement of our peace
was upon him; and with his stripes we are healed."

Please observe carefully the proofs listed by the Prophet Isaiah as
provided by Jesus in regard to His Messianic claims:

- He bore or shouldered our griefs and carried our sor-
rows to His cross;
- He didn't just verbalize empathy—He quite literally
took the load of all our disappointments upon himself;
- He was wounded (external) for our transgressions
(violations of God's commands);
- He was bruised (internal) for our iniquities (moral
impurities);
- The chastisement of our peace was upon Him; and,
- With His stripes we are healed.

This is what Jesus did for us at Calvary. This was the sacrifice that
was necessary for you and me to have peace. The cost for Jesus was the
mental and physical toll of being *stricken*, which literally means to be
afflicted with something overwhelming, as strong emotion or trouble.

Jesus vicariously took our place on the cross. Isaiah declared, "The
chastisement of our peace was upon Him." The key word is *chastisement*.
It comes from the Hebrew word *mucar*. As used in Isaiah 53:5, *mucar*,
according to *Vine's Expository Dictionary of Biblical Words*, means *the dis-
cipline or punishment meted out when one refuses to listen to instruction.*

Quite literally, the Prophet Isaiah is informing us that Jesus paid
the price so that we could still find peace, even though we originally
refused to obey the given instruction. What a Savior!

A Macro View of God's Peace

The Hebrew word for *peace* in Isaiah 53:5 is *shalom*. It literally
means *to destroy the authority of the one who binds us to chaos.* Jesus did
this for us. He destroyed the authority of the one who binds us to

chaos. No one in this world has to live in chaos anymore; Jesus paid the price for us to have peace.

A good transliteration of this word *peace* is *to sever the connection with chaos.* Jesus does this for persons who turn to Him with all of

A GOOD TRANSLITERATION OF THIS WORD PEACE IS TO SEVER THE CONNECTION WITH CHAOS

their heart and soul. He severs the connection to chaos.

Consider the episode revealed in Mark 4:39, which says,

> *"And he arose, and rebuked the wind, and said unto the sea, Peace, be still. And the wind ceased, and there was a great calm."*

His voice in our lives can still cause the wind to cease. He continues to replace great storms with a great calm. With those words, *"Peace, be still,"* the connection with chaos is effectively severed in our lives and minds.

The Master did this for the disciples in John 20:19:

> *"Then the same day at evening, being the first day of the week, when the doors were shut where the disciples were assembled for fear of the Jews, came Jesus and stood in the midst, and saith unto them, Peace be unto you."*

When some great personages step into a room, there is a sense of awe. When Jesus steps into our midst, there is not only that sense of profound awe, there is also a pervasive sense of a deep and abiding peace.

This was the very reason that Jesus Christ came in the flesh into this world. Luke gives this testimony in Luke 2:14, saying,

> *"Glory to God in the highest, and on earth peace, good will toward men."*

Jesus came in the flesh in order that *on earth* the authority of the one who binds us to chaos might be completely destroyed. He came to offer us *The Way* to sever our personal connection to chaos.

The Cost of Rejecting the Peace that God Gives

Our focus in this book is on God's mercy. Perhaps, though, we should briefly consider the fate of those who reject God's mercy and peace.

In Luke 19, Jesus viewed the city of Jerusalem and wept over it. Notice His lament in verse 42.

> *"If thou hadst known, even thou, at least in this thy day, the things which belong unto thy peace! but now they are hid from thine eyes."*

Jesus was distressed that Jerusalem was rejecting God's offer of peace. Notice what He predicted would follow this rejection of peace, recorded in Luke 19:43-44.

> *"For the days shall come upon thee, that thine enemies shall cast a trench about thee, and compass thee round, and keep thee in on every side,*
>
> *And shall lay thee even with the ground, and thy children within thee; and they shall not leave in thee one stone upon another; because thou knewest not the time of thy visitation."*

The price is always extremely high when a person rejects God's peace in his or her life. One reason that the price is so high is because such rejection is so senseless.

The Way to Peace

In Mark 5:34, Jesus spoke to the woman with the issue of blood. Traditional history tells us her name was Veronica. Pay close attention to Jesus' words to her: "And he said unto her, Daughter, thy faith hath made thee whole; go in peace, and be whole of thy plague."

The phrase go *in peace* catches my attention here. In the Greek, the phrase is literally *go into peace*. Jesus severed her connection to chaos. She would now have something new and extraordinary in her life. In her future there was a genuine opportunity for peace.

This is His offer to each of us. Read again John 14:27.

> *"Peace I leave with you, my peace I give unto you: not as the world giveth, give I unto you. Let not your heart be troubled, neither let it be afraid."*

Romans 14:17 gives us an additional understanding about this peace.

> *"For the kingdom of God is not meat and drink; but righteousness, and peace, and joy in the Holy Ghost."*

Acts 2:38 speaks to us as to how we should prepare to receive this peace found in the Holy Spirit.

> *"Then Peter said unto them, Repent, and be baptized every one of you in the name of Jesus Christ for the remission of sins, and ye shall receive the gift of the Holy Ghost."*

There are tremendous benefits for us in the peace that God gives. Consider with me the proclamation of the Apostle Paul in Philippians 4:7.

> *"And the peace of God, which passeth all understanding, shall keep your hearts and minds through Christ Jesus."*

In Acts 3:19, the Apostle Peter told an inquiring crowd these words of command and hope.

> *"Repent ye therefore, and be converted, that your sins may be blotted out, when the times of refreshing shall come from the presence of the Lord."*

The great news for those who are without the peace that God gives is that the door of old-fashioned repentance is still open. Mercy is still available. Today it is still open 24/7.

There is a day coming when the gate of mercy to the gospel will be closed. I urge you not to wait until it's too late to seek the Lord. Come to Him while mercy is still open for business.

Another songwriter of yesteryear, William R. Newell, summed it up in these melodious words:

> "Mercy there was great and grace was free,
> Pardon there was multiplied to me,
> There my burdened soul found liberty,
> At Calvary."

CHAPTER SIX

Mercy and the Unpardonable Sin

Mark 3:28-30 states:

> *"Verily I say unto you, All sins shall be forgiven unto the sons of men, and blasphemies wherewith soever they shall blaspheme:*
>
> *But he that shall blaspheme against the Holy Ghost hath never forgiveness, but is in danger of eternal damnation:*
>
> *Because they said, He hath an unclean spirit."*

The New Century Version says it this way:

> *"I tell you the truth. All sins that people do can be forgiven. And all the bad things people say against God can be forgiven.*
>
> *But anyone who says bad things against the Holy Spirit will never be forgiven. He is guilty of a sin that continues forever.*
>
> *Jesus said this because the teachers of the law said that Jesus had an evil spirit in him."*

In these three short verses of Scripture, there is both the threat of the most severe judgment and the offer of the most marvelous mercy. It is noteworthy that both *"hair-raising" fear* and *reassuring hope* are placed in such close proximity to one another in the textual landscape of the Bible.

It reminds me of the old picture of the great storm with its dark and foreboding clouds and the trees being harassed by strong winds. Over to the side is a large rock that looms tall. Under its overhang there is a small bird protected from the wind and the storm. It has its head thrown back, and it is singing. The painting is entitled "Peace."

I see a similar picture in these Bible verses. It is a scene of mercy in the shadow of severe judgment.

The main focus of this chapter will be on mercy. However, I do want to take a few lines and address this scariest of all earthly subjects; that is, the unpardonable sin.

The Unpardonable Sin

Although I could do so biblically, I will not take the time to prove all of my statements with reference to this sin. I will, however, highlight some issues and make some observations in regard to the sin that has no forgiveness.

The unpardonable sin can be an ongoing event and/or a progressive action. As such, it would be a continual and persistent resistance to the Holy Ghost. The stubborn resistance is maintained until a person dies, or is cut off by God; thus, an individual continually resisting the Holy Spirit runs out of opportunities to get right with God. Consequently, his or her obstinate rebellion is unpardonable.

Such persons resist the Holy Ghost. They continue their resistance until they grieve the Holy Ghost. Finally, they are eternally cut off from the Spirit of God. This is certainly one form of the unpardonable sin.

However, I don't believe that such definitions fully encompass the terrible and horrifying sin about which Jesus warned us. Also, is it possible that more than one type of action is, or can be, included in the unpardonable sin? Let's look at what the Bible has to say on this subject.

Matthew gives us an account of this teaching in chapter 12, verses 31-37, of his writings. The Pharisees accused Jesus of casting out devils through Beelzebub, the prince of devils. Jesus had declared in this same chapter that He cast out devils "by the Spirit of God," which is the Holy Ghost.

The Holy Ghost is God in action! In verse 31, Jesus calls the sin in question, "blasphemy against the Holy Ghost," or speaking against God in action. In verse 32, He classifies the guilty parties and the sin in this expression, "whosoever speaketh against the Holy Ghost." The language clearly delineates that this sin involves *speaking or talking;* namely, against the Holy Ghost (I will elaborate on this more shortly).

In verse 32, Jesus declares the severity of the Judgment on this sin,

> *"it shall not be forgiven him, neither in this world, neither in the world to come."*

If anything puts the fear of God in our hearts, this should.

Jesus made an additional and significant declaration in Luke 12:8-12.

> *Also I say unto you, Whosoever shall confess me before men, him shall the Son of man also confess before the angels of God:*
>
> *But he that denieth me before men shall be denied before the angels of God.*
>
> *And whosoever shall speak a word against the Son of man, it shall be forgiven him: but unto him that blasphemeth against the Holy Ghost it shall not be forgiven.*
>
> *And when they bring you unto the synagogues, and unto magistrates, and powers, take ye no thought how or what thing ye shall answer, or what ye shall say:*

> *For the Holy Ghost shall teach you in the same hour what ye ought to say.*

Here Jesus teaches on blasphemy of the Holy Ghost and links it with *denial*. Particularly, it is a denial "before men," or in front of others.

The connotation is a denial under pressure, for in the adjoining verse he speaks of the courts and the authorities and religious councils. According to the Lukan reference, such talk about the "Son of man" (reference to the flesh of God) is forgivable. Such talk against the Holy Ghost (God in action) is unforgivable.

It is questionable whether a person could deny the Holy Ghost in this fashion unless previously they had received the Holy Ghost. However, to have had the Holy Ghost and then to deny its reality is a most fearful thing indeed.

Mark gives us even more understanding on this awful sin in the third chapter of his book. There, Mark clearly notes (verse 30) why Jesus in verse 29 had given a warning of *eternal damnation* for blasphemers of the Holy Ghost—"Because they said, He hath an unclean spirit."

Who is the "they" referred to here? According to verse 22 it was the "scribes" or the religious teachers and recognized authorities of biblical interpretation. This is a significant fact.

They "came down from Jerusalem." Why would they make such an accusation? Verse 20 gives the reason for their coming and their concern, which led to their blasphemy; it was "the multitude."

Jesus was drawing humungous crowds. The scribes, speaking out against the miracles performed by Jesus and accusing Him of doing them by the power of the devil, were making *a deliberate attempt to cause other people to turn away from the Spirit of God.*

This, I believe, is the critical issue involved in the blasphemy of the Holy Ghost. It is a deliberate effort to cause other people to turn away from the Spirit of God. While I do believe we should be careful about any verbal reference to the Holy Ghost, I don't think the severe judgment attached to this warning is inclusive of people who have just voiced some personal doubt about the workings of God. Many persons have done that at some time in their life. Later they woke up to revelation, sought forgiveness for their folly, and it was granted. They are in church today and serving well. Some of them are now preachers.

The Apostle Paul was such a person. He spoke of himself in 1 Timothy 1:13, saying,

> *"Who was before a blasphemer, and a persecutor, and injurious: but I obtained mercy, because I did it ignorantly in unbelief."*

The key to his receiving forgiveness was that he was "ignorant" and in a state of "unbelief." This is radically different from *a deliberate and knowledgeable attempt* to turn people away from the Spirit of God.

This *willful blasphemy* is what Jesus had in mind when He spoke in Luke 17:1-2:

> *"Then said he unto the disciples, It is impossible but that offences will come: but woe unto him, through whom they come!*
>
> *It were better for him that a millstone were hanged about his neck, and he cast into the sea, than that he should offend one of these little ones."*

Unquestionably, the sin of blasphemy against the Holy Ghost is the most terrible thing a person can do. *Let us be warned and never encroach upon it.*

Marvelous Mercy

Note the reference to mercy—marvelous mercy—given right alongside of the warning concerning blasphemy in Mark 3:28-30 (NCV):

- *"All* sins that people *do* can be forgiven."
- *"And all* the bad things people *say* . . . can be forgiven."

Take a moment and catalogue with me a list of some of the bad things people can *do*.

- Murder
- Lust
- Fornication
- Adultery
- Homosexuality
- Bestiality
- Incest
- Rape
- Chemical addictions
- Robbery and thievery
- Cheating and fraud
- Betraying family and friends
- Anger and violence
- Idolatry
- Witchcraft
- Hatred
- Violence
- What else?

Now let us identify some of the evil things that people can *say*.

- Cursing
- Lying
- Slander
- Disrespect
- False doctrine
- What else?

The fact is this—if individuals repent, they can be forgiven of *all* these sins! Hallelujah!

The Bible declares this to be true. 1 John 5:7 says,

> *"But if we walk in the light, as he is in the light, we have fellowship one with another, and the blood of Jesus Christ his Son cleanseth us from all sins."*

Robert Lowry, a songwriter of some decades ago, worded it like this:

> What can wash away my sins?
> Nothing but the blood of Jesus.
> What can make me whole again?
> Nothing but the blood of Jesus.
>
> O! Precious is the flow
> That makes me white as snow,
> No other fount I know,
> Nothing but the blood of Jesus.

The blood of Jesus Christ washes away *all* of our sin. That is *marvelous mercy* indeed!

Now let us consider another classic scriptural illustration of mercy in the shadow of severe judgment.

Magnified Mercy

Sodom and Gomorrah were morally polluted cities. They were cities in which sexual perversion was rampant. Lot chose to live in the environment of this filthy metro area.

Lot was not in the place where he should have been. In great mercy, God sent a warning to Lot that judgment was soon to fall on these spiritually decadent municipalities. He even sent two heavenly envoys to assist Lot in getting out of the city and the immediate region.

Genesis 19: 15-20 illustrates this:

> *"And when the morning arose, then the angels hastened Lot, saying, Arise, take thy wife, and thy two daughters, which are here; lest thou be consumed in the iniquity of the city.*
>
> *And while he lingered, the men laid hold upon his hand, and upon the hand of his wife, and upon the hand of his two daughters;* **the LORD being merciful unto him**:

and they brought him forth, and set him without the city. [Emphasis added]

And it came to pass, when they had brought them forth abroad, that he said, Escape for thy life; look not behind thee, neither stay thou in all the plain; escape to the mountain, lest thou be consumed.

And Lot said unto them, Oh, not so, my Lord:

*Behold now, thy servant hath found grace in thy sight, and **thou hast magnified thy mercy**, which thou hast shewed unto me in saving my life; and I cannot escape to the mountain, lest some evil take me, and I die: [Emphasis added]*

Behold now, this city is near to flee unto, and it is a little one: Oh, let me escape thither, (is it not a little one?) and my soul shall live."

The language of the Bible is interesting; it says, "and while he [Lot] lingered." Lot knew he was not where he should be, but he still hesitated to fulfill the command of God.

The Bible declares that the angelic beings literally took Lot, his wife, and his daughters by the hand and authoritatively led them out of the city. The result was that Lot's life was spared and his soul lived. When I read this story, I am amazed at how patient and how merciful God was with Lot.

MERCIFUL LITERALLY MEANS FULL OF MERCY.

"The Lord being merciful unto him." This is the Bible's summation of the entire episode. Merciful literally means *full of mercy*. It was He who was and is full of mercy that spared Lot's life.

Lot's Testimony

Lot himself gave a testimony about these events. It was a threefold tribute to the Almighty. Lot said:

- Thy servant has found grace in Your sight;
- You have magnified Your mercy; and,
- You have saved my life.

Lot gave witness that, in God's granting grace to him and pre-serving his life, the Lord had magnified—or made more visible—His mercy to Lot. What a great observation.

God's mercy, in actuality, cannot be enlarged. However, there are providences that God bestows upon us from time to time that make His mercy loom larger and more visible to our view. These are truly awesome experiences that should fill our hearts with deep grati-tude. Such incidents help us to better understand just how merciful the Lord truly is.

A Personal Experience with Mercy

Some years ago I was urgently called to the hospital at the request of a dying man. I had known this man for more than 20 years and considered him a friend. This man had at one time known the Lord, but for the last several years of his life he had not walked with God. He was not a terrible person, but he himself acknowledged that he was not right with God. He sensed the end of his life was near.

When I stepped into the hospital room, my father and mother were already there. My father, a long-time pastor, was talking with the man. They had been conversing about death, and the man had expressed that he was not spiritually prepared to die; consequently, he was afraid of dying.

My father reminded the man that years ago he had obeyed the gospel. My father went on to tell our mutual friend that if he would repent to God and mean it sincerely from his heart, God would have mercy upon him, forgive him, and restore him.

I entered the conversation at that point. I called him by name and inquired, "Is there anything at all that troubles you? Is there any-thing specifically that's not right between you and God?" He said, "Yes." He then expressed the nature of the problem. As he proceeded, he was overcome by emotion and immediately began to call out to God with great earnestness for mercy and help.

As he prayed, I reminded him that God is indeed merciful. I encouraged him to allow God to renew him in the Holy Ghost. Something holy welled up from deep inside his spirit. Those in the room could sense that victory was near. Almost instantaneously, as my father and mother, his wife, and I prayed with him, he broke out speaking in a heavenly language. It was not a shallow experience. Over the next while, even after the rest of us had ceased praying, he would occasionally break forth again into that heavenly prayer language as he continued communicating with God.

I was reminded as I left the hospital that day of just how merciful the Lord is. That incident magnified God's mercy in my thinking. It has forever enlarged my view and understanding of the mercy of God. God will reach a long way to rescue somebody who will sincerely cry out to Him.

> GOD WILL REACH A LONG WAY TO RESCUE SOMEBODY WHO WILL SINCERELY CRY OUT TO HIM.

I am not suggesting that folks wait until their last few hours to call upon the Lord. As a matter of fact, don't take that horrible chance. Many people don't have lingering moments at the end of their lives during which to pray. Many are cut down even before they know what hit them. Many die with no warning and no space or time to repent.

What I am suggesting is this—God is more merciful than you or I can possibly fathom. Such is His magnified mercy.

Mercy—marvelous mercy—in the shadow of severe judgment!

CHAPTER SEVEN

Marvelous Mercy

Matthew 5:7 says,

> "Blessed are the merciful: for they shall obtain mercy."

In this verse, Jesus articulates a divine principle. It was in force in the Old Testament, but it was not verbalized until the New Testament.

According to the Master Teacher, Jesus Christ, the road to mercy is paved with mercy. The only guarantee of mercy for any person is to be merciful with others.

The Importance of Forgiveness

Matthew 6:12 says,

> "And forgive us our debts, as we forgive our debtors."

It is very significant that Jesus included a petition for forgiveness and an application of forgiveness in the model prayer that He prescribed. It is remarkable that the only part of the Lord's Prayer that Jesus commented on after the presentation was this portion having to do with forgiveness and mercy.

These arresting words are supplemental to the illustrative prayer taught by Jesus in Matthew 6:14-15:

"For if ye forgive men their trespasses, your heavenly Father will also forgive you:

But if ye forgive not men their trespasses, neither will your Father forgive your trespasses."

The startling truth that Jesus declared is that our receiving mercy is absolutely dependent upon our granting forgiveness.

Now let us consider a command of Christ with regard to mercy and judgment.

Judge Not

Matthew 7:1-5 (NIV) warns:

"Do not judge, or you too will be judged.

For in the same way you judge others, you will be judged, and with the measure you use, it will be measured to you.

Why do you look at the speck of sawdust in your brother's eye and pay no attention to the plank in your own eye?

How can you say to your brother, 'Let me take the speck out of your eye,' when all the time there is a plank in your own eye?

You hypocrite, first take the plank out of your own eye, and then you will see clearly to remove the speck from your brother's eye."

It is essential to understand that these statements were made to persons who had no authority or responsibility to judge others. It is a fact that some persons have been placed in positions where they have a God-given or God-supported responsibility to exercise judgment over others. This would include those vested with church authority or those in positions of civil authority. However, all such persons must avoid hypocrisy and judgmental attitudes.

Please observe the comparison that Jesus used between *a speck of sawdust* and *a plank*. A plank would typically be a 2' x 12' with a linear measurement of 10 feet or more. What a contrast between a plank and a mere speck of sawdust!

Imagine an ophthalmologist with a plank covering his or her own eye attempting to remove a speck of sawdust from a patient's eye. Absurdity! The Lord makes it clear that it is just as blatantly ridiculous for us to be nitpicking with a brother or sister when we know that we have inconsistencies or deficiencies in our own lives. We should also consider that it is possible that the speck of sawdust in our brother's eye, which is tormenting us, is just a particle hanging on the end of the plank in our own eye.

There is a clear line of demarcation between a judgmental attitude and *discernment*. It is important that we understand the difference.

We need discernment. Discerning of spirits is one of the spiritual gifts of the New Testament. Judging is *not* one of the listed spiritual gifts.

It is interesting that Jesus used the term *brother* in this discourse about avoiding being judgmental. The subtle message is that relationships should bring out the best in us and not the worst.

A Parable with a Focus on Forgiveness

In Matthew 18:21-35, we read:

> *"Then came Peter to him, and said, Lord, how oft shall my brother sin against me, and I forgive him? till seven times?*
>
> *Jesus saith unto him, I say not unto thee, Until seven times: but, Until seventy times seven.*
>
> *Therefore is the kingdom of heaven likened unto a certain king, which would take account of his servants.*

And when he had begun to reckon, one was brought unto him, which owed him ten thousand talents.

But forasmuch as he had not to pay, his lord commanded him to be sold, and his wife, and children, and all that he had, and payment to be made.

The servant therefore fell down, and worshipped him, saying, Lord, have patience with me, and I will pay thee all.

Then the lord of that servant was moved with compassion, and loosed him, and forgave him the debt.

But the same servant went out, and found one of his fellowservants, which owed him an hundred pence: and he laid hands on him, and took him by the throat, saying, Pay me that thou owest.

And his fellowservant fell down at his feet, and besought him, saying, Have patience with me, and I will pay thee all.

And he would not: but went and cast him into prison, till he should pay the debt.

So when his fellowservants saw what was done, they were very sorry, and came and told unto their lord all that was done.

Then his lord, after that he had called him, said unto him, O thou wicked servant, I forgave thee all that debt, because thou desiredst me:

Shouldest not thou also have had compassion on thy fellowservant, even as I had pity on thee?

And his lord was wroth, and delivered him to the tormentors, till he should pay all that was due unto him.

*So likewise shall my heavenly Father do also unto you,
if ye from your hearts forgive not every one his brother
their trespasses."*

Consider the contemporary values of this illustrative story. A talent of gold in biblical times would be worth today approximately $450,000 in US currency. So, 10,000 talents would be worth approximately $4,500,000,000!

To demonstrate the immensity of this debt, it should be understood that the total tax revenue of King Herod for this province for an entire year has been estimated at $40,500,000 in today's market. In other words, this man's debt was more than eleven times the yearly income of the provincial king. Yet, in the story, *he was forgiven in full* by the reigning monarch.

Anyone who has turned to Jesus for forgiveness has been forgiven a debt of insurmountable proportions. We had no way to pay. The Savior had compassion upon us and freely forgave us the entire sum of our sins. Oh, what a Savior! Marvelous mercy!

This forgiven man had a debtor who owed him 100 pence or denarii. This amount in today's market would be worth approximately $8,000 in US currency.

As small as this bill was by comparison, the forgiven man was unwilling to forgive, or to even wait for payment from his fellow debtor. Even though he had been forgiven well over 500,000 times as much debt personally, he now demanded immediate satisfaction of the debt owed to him. When it was not forthcoming, he had the offender cast into jail until the bill should be paid in full. Jesus made it abundantly clear that this was a spiritual atrocity in light of how much this man had been personally forgiven.

The final two verses of this scriptural story give us a stern and startling warning. Here it is overtly stated that the one and only thing that will ever cause God to reinstate something to our account, for which He has previously forgiven us, is our refusal to forgive our brothers, from our hearts, for their offenses committed against us.

An Old Testament Illustration of Mercy

We have briefly considered in an earlier chapter some of the grievous sins of King David. Let us now read God's reprimand to David through Nathan the prophet in 2 Samuel 12:9-13.

> *"Wherefore hast thou despised the commandment of the LORD, to do evil in his sight? thou hast killed Uriah the Hittite with the sword, and hast taken his wife to be thy wife, and hast slain him with the sword of the children of Ammon.*
>
> *Now therefore the sword shall never depart from thine house; because thou hast despised me, and hast taken the wife of Uriah the Hittite to be thy wife.*
>
> *Thus saith the LORD, Behold, I will raise up evil against thee out of thine own house, and I will take thy wives before thine eyes, and give them unto thy neighbour, and he shall lie with thy wives in the sight of this sun.*
>
> *For thou didst it secretly: but I will do this thing before all Israel, and before the sun.*
>
> *And David said unto Nathan, I have sinned against the LORD. And Nathan said unto David, The LORD also hath put away thy sin; thou shalt not die."*

King David had committed two capital offenses—adultery and murder—for which there was no provision in the Mosaic law for forgiveness; yet, David was forgiven right on the spot. This was so even though there was no sacrifice prescribed or afforded for such sins. How could this be? Was it because David was the king? Was He God's "pet"? Was God showing partiality? The answer to each of these questions is a firm "No."

Remember that David repented immediately upon being confronted by the prophet Nathan. He did not deny his sins. He did not turn on the man of God and execute him, as his kingly prerogative could have permitted.

He confessed his sins and openly repented of them. His stirring prayer of repentance is found in Psalm 51. Prayerfully read these portions of that prayer.

Psalm 51:1-2; 9-12 (Moffatt version) states:

> "O God, as thou art kind, have mercy upon me, in thy vast pity wipe out my offences,
>
> wash me from every stain of guilt, and purge me from my sin."
>
> "hide thy face from my sins, and wipe out all my guilt;
>
> make me a clean heart, O God, and put a new, steadfast spirit in me;
>
> banish me not from thy presence, deprive me not of thy sacred Spirit; gladden me with thy saving aid again, and give me a willing spirit as my strength."

But there is something more. Five years before, David had dealt with a person who was in line to be executed. Right on the spot David had pardoned him. The story is told in 2 Samuel 9:6-7.

> "Now when Mephibosheth, the son of Jonathan, the son of Saul, was come unto David, he fell on his face, and did reverence. And David said, Mephibosheth. And he answered, Behold thy servant!
>
> And David said unto him, Fear not: for I will surely shew thee kindness for Jonathan thy father's sake, and will restore thee all the land of Saul thy father; and thou shalt eat bread at my table continually."

Mephibosheth was a member of a family that had become traitors to King David. Ishbosheth, Saul's son, and numerous other family members had tried to resist King David from ruling over Israel. The practice in Israel in reference to traitors was as follows:

- Execute the traitor;
- Execute all members of the traitor's family;
- Confiscate all their family properties; and,
- Surrender the confiscated properties to the personal possession of the reigning king.

When Mephibosheth was led to King David, he was very afraid. However, David showed mercy by sparing Mephibosheth's life. Not only did David do that, he also restored all of Saul's family property to Mephibosheth.

David extended himself even more toward this seemingly doomed man. He provided Mephibosheth with a daily seat at the king's dinner table. It was literally a *mercy seat!*

GOD GRANTED MERCY TO DAVID BECAUSE DAVID WAS MERCIFUL TO SOMEONE ELSE WHO WAS IN LINE TO BE EXECUTED.

Little did David realize when he spared and restored Mephibosheth that just five years down the road he was going to need mercy. God granted mercy to David because David was merciful to someone else who was in line to be executed.

James 2:13 (Moffatt version) confidently declares,

> *"For the judgment will be merciless to the man who has shown no mercy—whereas **the merciful life will triumph in the face of judgment**." [Emphasis added]*

It is an eternal principle...*blessed are the merciful: for they shall obtain mercy.*

CHAPTER EIGHT

The Road to Mercy

Deuteronomy 19:1-4 (NIV) says:

> *"When the LORD your God has destroyed the nations whose land he is giving you, and when you have driven them out and settled in their towns and houses,*
>
> *then set aside for yourselves three cities centrally located in the land the LORD your God is giving you to possess.*
>
> *Build roads to them and divide into three parts the land the LORD your God is giving you as an inheritance, so that anyone who kills a man may flee there.*
>
> *This is the rule concerning the man who kills another and flees there to save his life—one who kills his neighbor unintentionally, without malice aforethought."*

It is important to observe that not only were the Israelites to provide three cities, and later three more, as cities of refuge, but they were also instructed by God to *build roads to them*. There was an understood inference with reference to these roads; they were to be *the best roads* in the whole country. This truth is readily noticeable in portions of some of the other translations of Deuteronomy 19:3.

- "You shall prepare the roads"—(RSV)

- "Thou shalt prepare thee a way"—(KJV)
- "You shall prepare roads for yourself"—(NKJV)
- "And keep the roads to these cities in good repair"—(TLB)

The understood intent of this command of the Eternal through Moses was that these roads were to be the "interstate highways" of that day and time. These thoroughfares were to be easily accessible. Bridges were to be built over all gorges and ditches. Signs were to be posted at all crossroads pointing out the most direct route to the nearest city of refuge.

The roads were to be checked regularly and frequently. This routine check was to make sure that these roads were free from obstacles, debris, and potholes. Any person fleeing for his life toward mercy needed a smooth highway in order to have the maximum opportunity to get to the city of refuge.

The road check and road maintenance was considered so important that it was assigned to the priests themselves. It was their duty to make sure that the road to mercy was smooth and clear, thus allowing a needy soul to make a hasty trip to the city of refuge.

Mercy in New Testament Times

The Church of Jesus Christ is the modern day city of refuge. This is made transparently clear from the apostle Paul's words in 2 Corinthians 5:16-20 (NIV):

> *"So from now on we regard no one from a worldly point of view. Though we once regarded Christ in this way, we do so no longer.*
>
> *Therefore, if anyone is in Christ, he is a new creation; the old has gone, the new has come!*
>
> *All this is from God, who reconciled us to himself through Christ and gave us the ministry of reconciliation:*

that God was reconciling the world to himself in Christ, not counting men's sins against them. And he has committed to us the message of reconciliation.

We are therefore Christ's ambassadors, as though God were making his appeal through us. We implore you on Christ's behalf: Be reconciled to God."

I wish to highlight the core of the above verses.

- The Church and its members are not to regard any person from a worldly point of view.
- In Christ, all disciples have themselves been made into a new creation (if He did it for you and me, He can do it for anybody who will come to Him!).
- All genuine disciples have been reconciled to God.
- The Church has been given the *ministry* of reconciliation.
- The Church has been given the *message* of reconciliation .
- The members of Christ's Church are to be ambassadors for Christ, appealing to all people to come to the Church (city of refuge) and be reconciled to the Lord Jesus Christ.

The church of Jesus Christ should excel in the offering and granting of mercy. *Mercy cannot be separated from the message and ministry of reconciliation!*

The apostolic ministry must take the lead today in making sure that the road to mercy in our churches is not obstructed. If the preachers proclaim and model mercy, the members of our churches will most likely follow the teaching and example of their shepherds. The Church must remain a fountain from which mercy flows in abundance.

Humanity needs *hope*. It is my deeply held conviction that one of my main duties as a minister of the gospel of Jesus Christ is to give people hope. Jesus came *not to condemn* the world, but rather that the world through Him *might be saved* (John 3:17).

THE CHURCH MUST NOT ONLY GIVE PEOPLE A FIRST CHANCE, IT MUST ALSO GIVE THEM SECOND, THIRD, AND MORE OPPORTUNITIES TO GET IT RIGHT WITH GOD.

The Church must not only give people a first chance, it must also give them second, third, and more opportunities to get it right with God. The apostle Paul clearly made this point in dealing with a sinful situation in the church at Corinth. Notice carefully the scriptural progression, recorded in 1 Corinthians 5:1-5; 9-11; 13b (NKJV):

"It is actually reported that there is sexual immorality among you, and such sexual immorality as is not even named among the Gentiles—that a man has his father's wife!

And you are puffed up, and have not rather mourned, that he who has done this deed might be taken away from among you.

For I indeed, as absent in body but present in spirit, have already judged (as though I were present) him who has so done this deed.

In the name of our Lord Jesus Christ, when you are gathered together, along with my spirit, with the power of our Lord Jesus Christ,

deliver such a one to Satan for the destruction of the flesh, that his spirit may be saved in the day of the Lord Jesus."

"I wrote to you in my epistle not to keep company with sexually immoral people.

The Road to Mercy

Yet I certainly did not mean with the sexually immoral people of this world, or with the covetous, or extortioners, or idolaters, since then you would need to go out of the world.

But now I have written to you not to keep company with anyone named a brother, who is sexually immoral, or covetous, or an idolater, or a reviler, or a drunkard, or an extortioner—not even to eat with such a person."

"...Therefore put away from yourselves the evil person."

In the above scriptures, Paul is emphatic that open sin is not to be tolerated in the church. However, in 2 Corinthians 2:5-11, he is just as emphatic that a repentant soul should be accepted back and given another opportunity to walk with God and in the fellowship of the church.

"But if any have caused grief, he hath not grieved me, but in part: that I may not overcharge you all.

Sufficient to such a man is this punishment, which was inflicted of many.

So that contrariwise ye ought rather to forgive him, and comfort him, lest perhaps such a one should be swallowed up with overmuch sorrow.

Wherefore I beseech you that ye would confirm your love toward him.

For to this end also did I write, that I might know the proof of you, whether ye be obedient in all things.

To whom ye forgive any thing, I forgive also: for if I forgave any thing, to whom I forgave it, for your sakes forgave I it in the person of Christ;

Lest Satan should get an advantage of us: for we are not ignorant of his devices."

77

Paul decreed that the repentant soul should be restored to the fellowship of the Body of Christ. He also noted that if the Church refuses to grant such mercy, satan gains a needless advantage against us. In plain language, *satan's work is more effective in an environment where there is the absence of mercy.* Think about that!

SATAN'S WORK IS MORE EFFECTIVE IN AN ENVIRONMENT WHERE THERE IS THE ABSENCE OF MERCY.

Even as merciless as the devil is, he gives people second chances to do wrong. This is clearly demonstrated in the story of Nebuchadnezzar and the three Hebrew children. When the three Hebrews refused to bow and worship the golden image the first time, King Nebuchadnezzar gave them a second opportunity to do so.

If the devil and his comrades give second chances and many more, should not the Church do even more when it comes to showing mercy? Yes! In the Church, the road to mercy should be a super-highway!

The following portion of the inscription at the base of the Statue of Liberty should also describe the Church's openness to the hurting of our lost world.

> "Give me your tired, your poor,
> Your huddled masses yearning to breathe free,
> The wretched refuse of your teeming shore.
> Send these, the homeless, tempest-tost to me,
> I lift my lamp beside the golden door!"

It is worth repeating. God's Church must excel in the offering and granting of mercy. The road to mercy leads straight to the Cross through the Church of Jesus Christ.

CHAPTER NINE

The Fairness of God

I stand in absolute awe of the fairness of Almighty God. Some may have an argument with God about His mercy and fairness—not me! Throughout history and the various dispensations of time, God has always operated toward humanity with an irreproachable impartiality and an impeccable standard of *fairness!*

Simon Peter's revelation in Acts 10: 34-36 is astounding.

> *"Then Peter opened his mouth, and said, Of a truth I perceive that God is no respecter of persons:*
>
> *But in every nation he that feareth him, and worketh righteousness, is accepted with him.*
>
> *The word which God sent unto the children of Israel, preaching peace by Jesus Christ: (he is Lord of all.)"*

God has many qualities, superior character traits, and profound abilities, but none of them contradicts His fairness.

Consider the Foreknowledge of God

According to Isaiah 46:10, God knows the *end* from the *beginning*. It is my theological conclusion that God knows right now whether you and I will individually be saved or lost forever in eternity. He knows how we will respond to the gospel.

Here is a key understanding—*God deals with you and me as if He does not know what our response is going to be.* His foreknowledge does not remove or replace His fairness. His fairness will give you and me every chance to be saved.

I knew a man many years ago that vouched that it is determined at one's birth whether or not a person is to be saved or lost. He personally refused to even visit a church worship service because he declared that from his birth it was predestined that he would be non-religious. This is human reasoning grappling to understand the complexity of the human soul. Sadly, he had reached a wrong conclusion.

The truth is that spiritually we are all *free moral agents.* We all have the *power of choice.* We can repent or not repent. We can choose to obey God's Word or to not obey God's Word. We can select to serve God, or we can decide not to serve God. It is up to us. God's *fairness* gives us choices!

The Greatest Illustration of God's Fairness

The greatest insight into the fairness of God is to look at the way Jesus Christ treated His eventual betrayer, Judas Iscariot.

Luke 6: 12-16 says:

> *"And it came to pass in those days, that he went out into a mountain to pray, and continued all night in prayer to God.*
>
> *And when it was day, he called unto him his disciples: and of them he chose twelve, whom also he named apostles;*
>
> *Simon, (whom he also named Peter,) and Andrew his brother, James and John, Philip and Bartholomew,*
>
> *Matthew and Thomas, James the son of Alphaeus, and Simon called Zelotes,*

80

And Judas the brother of James, and Judas Iscariot, which also was the traitor."

Judas Iscariot, who would turn out to be the traitor, was chosen by Jesus to be an apostle. He was given *the identical call* as Simon Peter and the other apostles. Judas Iscariot participated in the apostolic ministry. Jesus sent him, along with the other eleven disciples, to preach the Good News and to heal the infirmed. Note Luke 9:1-2:

"Then he called his twelve disciples together, and gave them power and authority over all devils, and to cure diseases.

And he sent them to preach the kingdom of God, and to heal the sick."

Amazingly, Judas Iscariot was even given a responsible position among the group of the disciples in John 12:3-6:

"Then took Mary a pound of ointment of spikenard, very costly, and anointed the feet of Jesus, and wiped his feet with her hair: and the house was filled with the odour of the ointment.

Then saith one of his disciples, Judas Iscariot, Simon's son, which should betray him,

Why was not this ointment sold for three hundred pence, and given to the poor?

This he said, not that he cared for the poor; but because he was a thief, and had the bag, and bare what was put therein."

Judas Iscariot was no less than the treasurer for the operating funds of Jesus and his disciples. Yet, he was a thief. And, *Jesus knew his flawed character when He placed him in the stated position.* Observe this fact in John 2:24-25:

*"But Jesus did not commit himself unto them, because he knew **all** men,*

And needed not that any should testify of man: for he knew what was in man." [Emphasis added]

Why would Jesus knowingly do such a thing? Of a lesser person than Christ, we would likely ascribe it to poor business acumen. However, with Jesus it was intentional. It was part and parcel of His overwhelming fairness. Judas Iscariot would never be able to protest with any validity that Jesus wasn't fair to him!

Jesus was so fair with Judas Iscariot that even on the night before the Crucifixion the other disciples didn't have any idea as to who the betrayer of Christ might be.

John 13:21-29 illustrates this point:

"When Jesus had thus said, he was troubled in spirit, and testified, and said, Verily, verily, I say unto you, that one of you shall betray me.

Then the disciples looked one on another, doubting of whom he spake.

Now there was leaning on Jesus' bosom one of his disciples, whom Jesus loved.

Simon Peter therefore beckoned to him, that he should ask who it should be of whom he spake.

He then lying on Jesus' breast saith unto him, Lord, who is it?

Jesus answered, He it is, to whom I shall give a sop, when I have dipped it. And when he had dipped the sop, he gave it to Judas Iscariot, the son of Simon.

after the sop Satan entered into him. Then said Jesus unto him, That thou doest, do quickly.

Now no man at the table knew for what intent he spake this unto him.

For some of them thought, because Judas had the bag, that Jesus had said unto him, Buy those things that we have need of against the feast; or, that he should give something to the poor."

Contrary to the practice of many leaders, Jesus did not inform the other disciples of Judas Iscariot's evil character behind Judas' back. Jesus would not give Judas the opportunity to say that he transgressed against Christ because his brethren had been prejudiced against him. Jesus had been so fair with Judas Iscariot that even when Jesus finally did publicly identify him as the betrayer, the disciples just could not comprehend it.

Some say that Judas could not have been forgiven for what he did in betraying Christ. Is that a fact? Or, is it possible that he received no forgiveness simply because he never asked for it?

It should be pointed out that Judas Iscariot and Simon Peter each made the biggest mistakes of their lives on the same night. Judas Iscariot never sought forgiveness. He simply determined his fate with his own hands by going to a lonely place and committing suicide. In contrast, Simon Peter also went to a lonely place; however, he fell down and wept in a prayer of deep repentance to God. He placed his fate in the hands of God.

Oh, the fairness of God!

Whosoever Will

In Revelation 22:16-17, we read:

"I Jesus have sent mine angel to testify unto you these things in the churches. I am the root and the offspring of David, and the bright and morning star.

And the Spirit and the bride say, Come. And let him that heareth say, Come. And let him that is athirst come. And whosoever will, let him take the water of life freely."

The final verses of this chapter record the last statements of Jesus in the Bible to the human race. Consider His three closing subjects in reverse order.

- "Surely I come quickly;"
- "Don't mess with My Word;" (Paraphrase), and
- "*Whoever* is thirsty can come to me."

The wondrous truth of the Gospel is that *anyone* may come to Jesus. This is true regardless of…

- Age;
- Race;
- Culture;
- Social status;
- Religious background; and,
- Current spiritual standing.

In Matthew 11:28, Jesus reiterated the same welcoming invitation, saying,

"Come unto me, all ye that labour and are heavy laden, and I will give you rest."

Jesus is so eternally fair. He desperately wants you to be saved. So much so that He shed His own blood at Calvary and gave His life to redeem you from the curse of sin.

Jesus will even throw roadblocks in your path in a serious effort to keep you from going to the lake of fire. If you or I are lost, we will have only ourselves to blame.

Such is the fairness of Almighty God.

CHAPTER TEN

A Time to Heal

Ecclesiastes 3:1-8 says:

"To every thing there is a season, and a time to every purpose under the heaven:

A time to be born, and a time to die; a time to plant, and a time to pluck up that which is planted;

A time to kill, and a time to heal; a time to break down, and a time to build up;

A time to weep, and a time to laugh; a time to mourn, and a time to dance;

A time to cast away stones, and a time to gather stones together; a time to embrace, and a time to refrain from embracing;

A time to get, and a time to lose; a time to keep, and a time to cast away;

A time to rend, and a time to sew; a time to keep silence, and a time to speak;

A time to love, and a time to hate; a time of war, and a time of peace."

These inspired writings are from the journal of King Solomon. There certainly is a poetic cadence in the flow of these observations about life and living. The particular times noted here each has its own significance.

The rhythm in this scriptural passage actually camouflages the real time involved in numerous of these events. The poetic flow nearly leaves us with a feeling or notion that these are momentary times or times of short duration. The reality is that some of these times are momentary or short-lived while others are times that stretch over months or even a period of years.

A Contrast in Time

One of the obvious differences in consumable time is found in the first portion of verse seven of the previous-referenced scriptures; namely, there is "A time to rend, and a time to sew." The two times mentioned are not equal in duration. Ask any mother who has ever had to mend some of her children's clothing, torn while the child played, and she will quickly verify to you that it takes longer to sew a garment than it takes to tear it. An item of clothing can be torn in a split second, but it may require nine hundred times that long or more to repair and sew it.

When I was a child, my mother occasionally declared to me that I was able to mess things up faster than she could clean them up. I'm quite sure that I'm not the only person who has ever been so informed. It is evident that some things involve only a few moments of time, while others encompass a prolonged time.

Ponder for a few moments the contrast in the times listed in the latter segment of verse 3; specifically, "a time to break down, and a time to build up." Those of us who have observed large construction projects know that it can sometimes take several years to complete an expansive and complex facility. In contrast, a mammoth building can be brought down in a few weeks with cranes and wrecking balls. It can also be imploded and brought down in a matter of minutes with some well-placed and sequential explosives. The indubious point is that it takes much more time to build something of value than it does to tear it down.

This same enlightenment is true of our personal testimony and influence as a Christian. It often takes years to build credibility and powerful influence for Christ. That testimony, however, can be largely and quickly destroyed by a few moments of reckless living or a one night fling or binge. Think of it! A lifetime of Christian witness can be decimated in one evening of wickedness.

Healing

Reflect now on the declaration in verse 3, which notes that there is "a time to heal." This notation intrigues me.

Most Christians like to think in terms of the miraculous. We like to think in terms of that which is instantaneous. I unashamedly admit that I personally believe in the resolute and unquestionable power of Almighty God. He can do in a moment of time that which defies explanation and which is beyond human intelligence. You and I may not understand it, but there is an Unseen Hand that can move into the world of natural laws and bring about a supernatural miracle! I believe that with all my heart!

But the fact is that not everybody gets healed instantaneously. That is the naked truth. We believers usually don't like to talk about that case as much.

Rightfully, we get excited over stories of miraculous and instantaneous deliverance. We don't usually get very excited about long periods of recuperation and healing. The fact remains, all healing is not instantaneous. Some healing is immediate, but most healing happens over time. It may be that the time required is only a few days or weeks. Then again, healing may happen over a period of years—sometimes many years. The time can vary for us to be healed:

- Physically;
- Emotionally;
- Mentally;
- Socially;
- Financially; and/or,
- Spiritually.

We of the western world live in a society in which one of the key words is *hurry!* The routine for many could best be described as, "hurry to work, hurry home, hurry to eat, hurry to church or to some other meeting, and then hurry home to catch some sleep so we can do it all again the next day."

Ours is certainly a jet-paced society. We now consider microwave ovens a necessity. We want instant oatmeal, potatoes, and popcorn. Fast food restaurants are now a multi-billion dollar industry. We are consumers, and we want it available in a hurry.

THE BIBLE ITSELF INSTRUCTS OF THE NEED TO WAIT UPON THE LORD.

The plain truth is that *hurry* is often an enemy to the hand of God at work in our lives. The Bible itself instructs of the need to *wait upon the Lord*.

This instruction is not in opposition to faith. Reach for the stars! Reach for your miracle! Let your faith be exercised! Let your faith reach out to God! But if your healing doesn't happen in a moment, *don't give up!* There is a time to heal!

God did not express precisely the amount of time; He just notifies us that there is *a time to heal*. Sometimes it does take time. It is best if you and I just Jesus and leave the timing up to Him.

A Season

It is most interesting that when the preacher of Ecclesiastes spoke concerning the *times* in our lives, he also used the terminology *a season*. Read again the words, "To every thing there is a season."

This term in of itself indicates that some matters of life cover an extended period of time. For these matters, God grants us seasons.

According to Genesis 1:14, the very concept of seasons is God's idea. Seasons speak of the great patience of our loving and merciful Lord. He is patient with sinners, patient with young Christians, and patient and merciful to veteran Christians who are still a distance from perfection.

We must also respect the seasons in the lives of others. If we have advanced in our walk with the Lord, we must remember that we did not get to where we are in God overnight. God has been merciful and given us time to develop. We must be merciful to other people and give them time to mature in Christ. I remember our Lord saying, "Blessed are the merciful, for they shall obtain mercy" (Matthew 5:7). We need to express to others the compassion, patience, and understanding that we have received—and also need—from God.

Consider the manner of God's dealing with the wicked sinners of the world in the days of Noah. It is recorded in 1 Peter 3:20, which says,

> "Which sometime were disobedient, when once the long-suffering of God waited in the days of Noah, while the ark was a preparing, wherein few, that is, eight souls were saved by water."

God was disturbed greatly and moved to action with unregenerate and unrepentant humans of that era. Yet, He waited and refrained from judgment while the ark was being prepared—a period of at least 100 years. During the century or so that it took for the ark's construction, Noah preached to the citizens, thus giving them the opportunity to repent and be spared. It was God's mercy that gave the people such a long season to repent. O, the mercy of God!

I meet some folks who are insistent upon receiving justice. If we truly received justice, we would be blown away. The psalmist said it right in Psalm 130:3:

"If thou, LORD, shouldest mark iniquities, O Lord, who shall stand?"

Our hope is in God's mercy. It is not justice that we should cry out for; it is God's marvelous mercy. In the very next statement of the sweet psalmist of Israel, he points to God's mercy as our beacon of hope:

"But there is forgiveness with thee, that thou mayest be feared."

The writer then reiterates the concept of waiting on God. Notice this carefully in Psalm 130:5-6:

"I wait for the LORD, my soul doth wait, and in his word do I hope.

My soul waiteth for the Lord more than they that watch for the morning: I say, more than they that watch for the morning."

Then comes the psalmist's triumphant exclamation in Psalm 130:7-8:

"Let Israel hope in the LORD: for with the LORD there is mercy, and with him is plenteous redemption.

And he shall redeem Israel from all his iniquities."

With some persons, there is not much mercy. But with the Lord, there is plenteous mercy. I love it! With the Lord, there is copious redemption. And when Christ redeems and forgives, it is from *all* iniquities!

It is my personal and deeply held conviction that the Holy Spirit does not depart instantly from a believer's life upon the happening of some transgression or sin. As scriptural proof, I offer for your review the very words of Jesus related by the apostle John recorded in Revelation 2:21.

"And I gave her space to repent of her fornication; and she repented not."

The reference in the above verse was to a carnal prophetess who operated and hindered in the church of Thyatira, which was located in Asia Minor (modern Turkey). It must not be overlooked, though her influence was very unholy, God gave her a space, a measure of time, a season, in which to repent. It was only after her clearly demonstrated unwillingness to repent that the Lord flung her into severe judgment.

I truly believe that when individuals fail, the good Lord gives them space, or a season, to repent. God gives them time to see their wrong and to get it right. Only in the face of an outright refusal to repent will the Holy Spirit depart from a believer's life. Jesus himself promised that all that come to Him in repentance and obedience He will in no wise cast out (John 6:37).

God is not a mean ogre with a billy club just waiting for people to mess up so He can bash them. The truth is that He is more merciful than human beings can comprehend and understand.

If you have messed up morally or spiritually, you have no doubt received counsel from the archenemy of your soul to just "throw in the towel" and quit even trying to live for God. That is not good advice.

What you must do is turn from your error and transgression and fall before the Lord Jesus in deep repentance. If you mean it, He will grant you marvelous mercy and forgive you. He will enable you, perhaps through other helpful Christians, to be restored.

Thank God that He gives *a time to heal*. Oh, marvelous mercy!

---·•·---

CHAPTER ELEVEN

---·•·---

His Mercy Is Everlasting

Psalm 100:4-5 proclaims:

> *"Enter into his gates with thanksgiving, and into his courts with praise: be thankful unto him, and bless his name.*

> *For the LORD is good; his mercy is everlasting; and his truth endureth to all generations."*

In verse four of Psalm 100, God's people are given four distinct commands:

- Enter His gates with thanksgiving;
- Enter His courts with praise;
- Be thankful unto Him; and,
- Bless His name.

The clarion message is that each worshiper who comes through the doors and enters the sanctuary of God's House should give the Lord thanks and praise. The worshipper is to bless (or glorify) and exalt the Lord's name. It is also noted that the worshipper is to *be* thankful. Thankfulness is not to be just a momentary experience at church. It must be an attitude and a lifestyle that is maintained constantly.

Verse five gives us three stupendous reasons why we should fulfill the commands of verse four:

- The Lord is good;
- His mercy is everlasting; and,
- His truth endureth to all generations.

Here is the basis for worship. God is good—all the time. All the time—God is good. His truth never flags. And then there is His mercy. *His mercy is everlasting.* Think about it for a moment. It is indeed *marvelous mercy!*

GOD IS GOOD — ALL THE TIME.

Let's take a closer look at the *everlasting* quality of God's mercy.

The Bible Does *Not* Say that God's Mercy is Eternal

Eternal means having infinite duration, continued without intermission: perpetual. More specifically, it means *without a beginning or an ending.*

God *is* eternal. He had no beginning, and He has no ending. His moral attributes never change, such as His love, goodness, fairness, impartiality, etc.

However, there are relational aspects of God that are *not* eternal. God is capable of entering new relationships with His creation as time goes along. With each new relationship, God acquires a new title, but this does not change His essence nor pluralize the one God.

The declaration of Deuteronomy 6:4 will never be modified, "Hear, O Israel: The Lord our God is one LORD."

However, God's mercy is *not* eternal. Nowhere in the Bible does it reference God's mercy as being *eternal.* Were it eternal, it would be automatic. If God's mercy were eternal, no one would ever have to repent and request mercy.

The truth is that all mercy has a beginning. It must be requested. It is placed in operation when a person repents and asks God for forgiveness.

Though His Mercy is Not Eternal, It is *Everlasting*

Mercy has a point of origination. Subsequently, once mercy is extended, it never weakens. Mercy never fades. God's mercy never loses its efficacy or effectiveness. *His mercy endureth forever!*

There is only one condition noted in the Bible where mercy can ever be withdrawn, and that is if we refuse to forgive a fellow human being of an offense they have committed against us. Other than that, once mercy is applied it remains perpetually in effect. One can never be charged with that particular offense again. There is no "double jeopardy" with God.

Here is an illustration of this principle. Supposing someone tells a lie today. Later this evening or tomorrow, their conscience is smitten. They go to the deceived party and correct the false statement. Then they go to God in a prayer of sincere repentance. Mercy is applied. Here, then, is the awesome conclusion. No matter what other sins they commit after that, including telling another lie, God will never go back and charge them again with the earlier falsehood. *His mercy is everlasting!*

For His Mercy Endureth Forever

Psalm 136 is a unique chapter of the Holy Bible. Each of its twenty-six verses ends with the same exact expression. It is for deliberate emphasis that all the verses of Psalm 136 end with the proclamation, "for his mercy endureth for ever."

This is the only time in Scripture that one particular truth is so often repeated in a single chapter. This precise message is repeated no less than 35 times in the Bible, and 26 of the declarations are found in Psalm 136. This is a maxim that God does not want us to miss. This drill of repetition is God's method of stamping this important message into our brains.

Psalm 136:1 is a divine recipe that produces tremendous spiritual energy and power. When any person begins to fulfill this command with sincerity, there is a spiritual force released that is greater than the electricity produced by a gigantic dam or a hydroelectric plant. I repeat, this passage is a reservoir of spiritual energy and power.

Allow me to illustrate. Consider the dedication of Solomon's Temple as recorded in 2 Chronicles 5:11-14:

> *"And it came to pass, when the priests were come out of the holy place: (for all the priests that were present were sanctified, and did not then wait by course:*
>
> *Also the Levites which were the singers, all of them of Asaph, of Heman, of Jeduthun, with their sons and their brethren, being arrayed in white linen, having cymbals and psalteries and harps, stood at the east end of the altar, and with them an hundred and twenty priests sounding with trumpets:)*
>
> *It came even to pass, as the trumpeters and singers were as one, to make one sound to be heard in praising and thanking the LORD; and when they lifted up their voice with the trumpets and cymbals and instruments of musick, and praised the LORD, saying, For he is good; for his mercy endureth for ever: that then the house was filled with a cloud, even the house of the LORD;*
>
> *So that the priests could not stand to minister by reason of the cloud: for the glory of the LORD had filled the house of God."*

Observe carefully that this was during the Dedication Service. The implementation of the formula given in Psalm 136:1 in the worship service brought an awesome and visible manifestation of God's glory. In fact, the cloud of glory was so thick that the priests had to step back for awhile and just let God be God.

"For His mercy endureth for ever." Just what does this statement mean?

1. Does it mean that a person can live an evil life and not fear the consequences of judgment?
2. Does it mean that mercy will always be available for the sinner or backslider?

The answer to both questions is absolutely *no!*

Endureth means *to continue in existence, to last,* or *everlasting.*

- His mercy continues in existence forever;
- His mercy is lasting; and,
- His mercy is everlasting.

The correct understanding of the proclamation is this:

- Once God extends mercy for an offense, that mercy never weakens nor crumbles.
- God's mercy always continues to triumph over offenses and judgment.
- That granted mercy remains effective and in force for all eternity.
- God's mercy never loses its efficaciousness, nor its power.

These thoughts are in line with the awesome and inspiring verses of Lamentations 3:21-26.

"This I recall to my mind, therefore have I hope.

It is of the LORD's mercies that we are not consumed, because his compassions fail not.

They are new every morning: great is thy faithfulness.

The LORD is my portion, saith my soul; therefore will I hope in him.

The LORD is good unto them that wait for him, to the soul that seeketh him.

It is good that a man should both hope and quietly wait for the salvation of the LORD."

Another fact we need to understand is this—you and I can add fresh offenses, which are not covered, nor pardoned, by the gift of God's *past* mercies to us. In the case of a new offense or sin, you and I must go to God *again* in repentance, which includes getting the sin out of our lives. When this is done properly and sincerely, God grants new and fresh mercy.

Acts 3:19 states it like this:

"Repent ye therefore, and be converted, that your sins may be blotted out, when the times of refreshing shall come from the presence of the Lord."

Note the phrase "the times of refreshing." This is something God desires to send to every person. There is no refreshing in the entire world that can compare to the refreshing God can give to the human soul. According to the above verse of scripture, this refreshing comes from the presence of the Lord. However, it is imperative to observe that it only comes after *repentance* and *conversion*.

God's Mercy is Extended to the Repentant Soul Immediately

Many of us can forgive, providing enough time has passed to take the edge off of the offense. Some folks forgive things in the distant past, but they refuse to forgive trespasses in the present.

Many of us hold no ill will toward King David for his adultery and murder because it was committed centuries ago. And yet, we do not truly forgive people we know who have committed adultery or other hurtful offenses.

God's mercy is so awesome! He forgives in the *present!* Carefully note these biblical examples.

In 2 Samuel 12, the prophet Nathan confronted David about his sins. David's response in verse 13 was, *"I have sinned against the Lord."* Nathan's response in the very same verse was, *"The Lord also hath put away thy sin."* Note that mercy was *immediate.*

In Luke 23, the historical record is given of Jesus hanging on the cross and looking directly in the face of his executors. He then uttered this profound intercession for them, "Father, forgive them [now]; for they know not what they do." His proffered mercy was immediate.

God's Mercy Leaves No Stigma or Taint on the Forgiven

Some forgive, but they never let the forgiven forget the failure. Jesus truly forgives and forgets. The Lord proclaimed in Isaiah 43:25,

> *"I, even I, am he that blotteth out thy transgressions for mine own sake, and will not remember thy sins."*

God forgives *thoroughly* and *completely.* He *removes all* of sin's stains. He leaves no reminders on the soul of the penitent.

Consider this biblical illustration of that glorious fact. In John 8, a woman caught *in the very act* of adultery was brought to Jesus. **GOD FORGIVES THOROUGHLY AND COMPLETELY.** After inquiring about her accusers, Jesus responded, "Neither do I condemn thee: go, and sin no more."

Observe that Jesus did *not* say, "Neither do I condemn adultery." He *does* condemn adultery. However, Jesus did not have a condemning attitude towards the woman. Forgiveness to her was immediate, and He twisted no knife into her soul to constantly remind her of her past shame. The Lord Jesus gave her the chance to start over without having to live under a stigma and condemnation from God.

Wow! His mercy is everlasting!

CHAPTER TWELVE

Perfected Forever

Song of Solomon 4:7 says,

"Thou art all fair, my love; there is no spot in thee."

In other words, the songwriter declares of his lover that she is perfect. Now, this was not an expression of some man fantasizing. The king, the husband, made this statement. It was said about his bride, his wife, with whom he had been intimate. He stated that she was all fair and without spot, blemish, or flaw.

The Song of Solomon is a love story in the Old Testament. The significance is that it actually reveals to us in poetic form the love that Christ has for His Church. It expresses by analogy the way God feels about His Church.

Against this backdrop, reflect upon the words of the writer Jude in the New Testament in Jude 24-25:

"Now unto him that is able to keep you from falling, and to present you faultless before the presence of his glory with exceeding joy,

To the only wise God our Saviour, be glory and majesty, dominion and power, both now and ever. Amen."

View again the phrase, "and to present you faultless before the presence of his glory with exceeding joy." God, our Savior, is able to present you faultless before the presence of His glory.

God has the ability to present His Church, and the individual member, before His presence, totally and completely without fault!

This is nothing short of a miracle. In fact, there are three miracles in this verse. God is able to:

- Keep us from falling;
- Present us faultless; and,
- Enable us to finish our race with exceeding joy.

I can scarcely contain it. He is able to keep you and me from falling. What a miracle! Our journey will not end in bitterness and defeat. Another miracle! But right in the middle of those two is another miracle. He is able to present us *faultless* before the presence of His glory!

GOD HAS THE ABILITY TO PRESENT HIS CHURCH, AND THE INDIVIDUAL MEMBER, BEFORE HIS PRESENCE, TOTALLY AND COMPLETELY WITHOUT FAULT!

Now the truth is all the more astounding when we pause long enough to remember that, as a matter of fact, we do have faults. Even ministers have faults. God has a marvelous ability through His mercy and His grace to actually present us before the presence of His glory without a fault! Wow!

Regeneration

The process of individual transformation toward perfection all begins with what is often referred to as the new birth, being born from above, or being born again. Jesus made this dramatic change possible through His suffering and death on Calvary. A sinner can be spiritually regenerated into a new creation.

This is the precise message of the great missionary and apostle in 1 Corinthians 6:9-11.

> *"Know ye not that the unrighteous shall not inherit the kingdom of God? Be not deceived: neither fornicators, nor idolaters, nor adulterers, nor effeminate, nor abusers of themselves with mankind,*
>
> *Nor thieves, nor covetous, nor drunkards, nor revilers, nor extortioners, shall inherit the kingdom of God.*
>
> *And such were some of you: but ye are washed, but ye are sanctified, but ye are justified in the name of the Lord Jesus, and by the Spirit of our God."*

Look at the list of those who are prohibited from inheriting the kingdom of God. Most of us at some time in our lives have found ourselves in at least one place on this list.

- Unrighteous
- Fornicators
- Idolaters
- Adulterers
- Effeminate
- Homosexuals
- Thieves
- Greedy
- Drunkards
- Slanderers
- Swindlers

Then comes the phrase, "And such *were* some of you." [Emphasis added] Oh, the mercy of God! He washed us! He cleansed us! He took it all away! He sanctified us! He justified us! And here are the power tools that liberated us and gave us a place in the Bride of Christ. We are sanctified and justified:

- In the name of the Lord Jesus and
- By the Spirit of our God.

Isaiah gives witness to God's mercy in chapter 43:25:

> *"I, even I, am he that blotteth out thy transgressions for mine own sake, and will not remember thy sins."*

Read it again. The Lord clearly stated that He took this redeeming action "for [His] own sake." He did it just because He wanted to do so. He did it because of His awesome love for people.

Then the Lord added a most magnificent warranty. He boldly asserted that He would not remember our forgiven sins! That is phenomenal! We have an ability that God chooses not to exercise. We can remember some things that we previously did which are now under the blood. However, God doesn't remember those things of which we have repented and that He has forgiven. There is wonder working power in the blood of the Lamb!

Consider with me the following additional evidence from Romans 5:6-11:

> *"For when we were yet without strength, in due time Christ died for the ungodly.*
>
> *For scarcely for a righteous man will one die: yet peradventure for a good man some would even dare to die.*
>
> *But God commendeth his love toward us, in that, while we were yet sinners, Christ died for us.*
>
> *Much more then, being now justified by his blood, we shall be saved from wrath through him.*
>
> *For if, when we were enemies, we were reconciled to God by the death of his Son, much more, being reconciled, we shall be saved by his life.*
>
> *And not only so, but we also joy in God through our Lord Jesus Christ, by whom we have now received the atonement."*

The poignant point is this: He loved us enough to die for us while we were yet sinners. All the more, He will save us from wrath because we have been justified by His blood! Hallelujah!

The Washing of Water by the Word

Ephesians 5:25-27 says:

"Husbands, love your wives, even as Christ also loved the church, and gave himself for it;

That he might sanctify and cleanse it with the washing of water by the word,

That he might present it to himself a glorious church, not having spot, or wrinkle, or any such thing; but that it should be holy and without blemish."

Focus for a moment on the phrase "the washing of water by the word." The Word of God has a cleansing effect upon a true Christian. One of the things that transpire while we're in church is that we get a spiritual bath or shower. There is a spiritual washing that takes place in our lives through the preaching of the Word of God. We are also sanctified, or set apart for the Master's service, by that same anointed preaching and teaching of the Word of God.

> **THE WORD OF GOD HAS A CLEANSING EFFECT UPON A TRUE CHRISTIAN.**

The reason for this washing, cleansing, and sanctification is revealed in verse 27, "That he might present it to himself a glorious church, not having spot, or wrinkle, or any such thing; but that it should be holy and without blemish." It is important to notice that His bride will be holy and without flaw. Remember, the Church is a gift that God is giving himself. He doesn't give us junk, and neither will He give himself something that is all ravaged, torn, or scarred. The Church will not be disfigured. It will be a glorious Church.

The apostle Paul emphasized in Ephesians 5 that when Christ presents the Church unto himself, it will be without even a spot. What are spots? There are actually two kinds of spots.

First of all, the word in the Greek that is translated spot can also correctly be translated as *fault*. Thus, it would be appropriate to say that the presented Church will be without fault. A *fault* is *an inherent or an innate flaw*. As such, it speaks of something intrinsically or internally defective. God's Church will be neither deficient nor defective. It will be a glorious Church!

Secondly, there is another kind of spot. These are the spots that a Christian picks up as he or she walks through this world. These spots are the residue and stains that the world leaves on us in our everyday living. However, God has a washing process. The Lord God has a cleansing and sanctifying process in which He can absolutely bleach out every spot whether it is an inward fault or an outward stain. The reigning Church will not be spotted. It will be pure and triumphant.

Paul also stipulates that the presented Church will be free of any wrinkles. The Church of Jesus Christ will be ageless and forever youthful. It will not be wrinkled and deteriorating. God's Church will be victorious!

This reference to the lack of wrinkles is also, no doubt, a notation of the superb condition of the attire of the Bride of Christ—the Church. How does a bride get wrinkles in her wedding gown? It happens just by sitting on it. God's Bride will not have wrinkles in her wedding gown because she is not just a sitting showpiece. She is an active agent in this world, attending to the business of the Bridegroom. The Church will rule and reign with Christ.

To this, the Apostle John adds his testimony in 1 John 1:7, saying,

"But if we walk in the light, as he is in the light, we have fellowship one with another, and the blood of Jesus Christ his Son cleanseth us from all sin."

The blood of Jesus does not just sprinkle or splatter us. It flows and it *cleanses*. To *cleanse* is to *remove every particle of toxin or filth*. The blood of Jesus Christ cleanses us from all sin!

Sometimes it is difficult for us to fully connect with these truths. The reason is often because we know ourselves so well. We know our many imperfections. However, the Word of God stands true regardless of human frailty and weakness. The blood of Jesus Christ cleanseth us from all sin!

Perfection Forever

This matter of cleansing and perfection is also addressed in Hebrews 10:1-4; 9-23:

"For the law having a shadow of good things to come, and not the very image of the things, can never with those sacrifices which they offered year by year continually make the comers thereunto perfect.

For then would they not have ceased to be offered? because that the worshippers once purged should have had no more conscience of sins.

But in those sacrifices there is a remembrance again made of sins every year.

For it is not possible that the blood of bulls and of goats should take away sins."

"Then said he, Lo, I come to do thy will, O God. He taketh away the first, that he may establish the second.

By the which will we are sanctified through the offering of the body of Jesus Christ once for all.

And every priest standeth daily ministering and offering oftentimes the same sacrifices, which can never take away sins:

But this man, after he had offered one sacrifice for sins for ever, sat down on the right hand of God;

From henceforth expecting till his enemies be made his footstool.

For by one offering he hath perfected for ever them that are sanctified.

Whereof the Holy Ghost also is a witness to us: for after that he had said before,

This is the covenant that I will make with them after those days, saith the Lord, I will put my laws into their hearts, and in their minds will I write them;

And their sins and iniquities will I remember no more.

Now where remission of these is, there is no more offering for sin.

Having therefore, brethren, boldness to enter into the holiest by the blood of Jesus,

By a new and living way, which he hath consecrated for us, through the veil, that is to say, his flesh;

And having an high priest over the house of God;

Let us draw near with a true heart in full assurance of faith, having our hearts sprinkled from an evil conscience, and our bodies washed with pure water.

Let us hold fast the profession of our faith without wavering; (for he is faithful that promised.)"

Under the law, sins were simply rolled ahead for one year. Animal sacrifices could not remove sin; they could only roll them forward. On the next anniversary, the sins had to be confronted and dealt with again. The priests had to continually repeat their sacrifices to deal with the ongoing problem of sin. However, the sacrifice of Jesus is efficacious *forever* because He does not just roll sins ahead. *He expunges and removes them, leaving not a trace!* Oh, the marvelous mercy of God!

It is interesting wording in verse 13 that notes Jesus is "expecting." Just what is our Lord expecting? The answer is given in the same brief verse, "till his enemies be made his footstool." To say it another way, He is expecting complete subjugation of His enemies and total triumph for His Church.

Verse 14 uses the word "perfected" with reference to the Church of Jesus Christ. The world is going down, the devil is going to hell, but the Church is going to be presented to God without fault—perfect!

Verses 15 and 16 make it plain that the Holy Ghost is a witness to God's work of sanctification within our lives and to our ultimate destiny of eternal victory. Verse 19 stipulates that we have "boldness" (could also be translated "liberty") to enter the Holy of Holies through, or because of, the blood of Jesus.

In the Old Testament, the only person allowed to enter the Holy of Holies in the Tabernacle was the High Priest. A person could not become the High Priest if he

THE BLOOD OF JESUS CLEANSES AND SANCTIFIES US AND LEAVES US FLAWLESS!

had any flaw or defect whatsoever. He had to be a perfect physical specimen. However, in the New Testament, all true believers may come into the very Holy of Holies. How is this made possible? The blood of Jesus cleanses and sanctifies us and leaves us flawless!

Oh, marvelous mercy!

CHAPTER THIRTEEN

The Reach of Mercy

Just how tall is God's mercy? Did you ever contemplate the height of God's mercy? How far can the mercy of God reach? How much grip is there in His hands?

Psalm 103:1-4; 8-19 says:

"Bless the LORD, O my soul: and all that is within me, bless his holy name.

Bless the LORD, O my soul, and forget not all his benefits:

Who forgiveth all thine iniquities; who healeth all thy diseases;

Who redeemeth thy life from destruction; who crowneth thee with lovingkindness and tender mercies."

"The LORD is merciful and gracious, slow to anger, and plenteous in mercy.

He will not always chide: neither will he keep his anger forever.

He hath not dealt with us after our sins; nor rewarded us according to our iniquities.

For as the heaven is high above the earth, so great is his mercy toward them that fear him.

As far as the east is from the west, so far hath he removed our transgressions from us.

Like as a father pitieth his children, so the LORD pitieth them that fear him.

For he knoweth our frame; he remembereth that we are dust.

As for man, his days are as grass: as a flower of the field, so he flourisheth.

For the wind passeth over it, and it is gone; and the place thereof shall know it no more.

But the mercy of the LORD is from everlasting to everlasting upon them that fear him, and his righteousness unto children's children;

To such as keep his covenant, and to those that remember his commandments to do them.

The LORD hath prepared his throne in the heavens; and his kingdom ruleth over all."

The psalmist reminds us in verse two of the awesome benefits package that comes with being a child of God. In verse three it is declared that the Lord forgiveth *all* our iniquities and that He is the Healer of every disease. Verse four speaks of God's physical protection, His "lovingkindness" (Old Testament word for "grace"), and the Lord's "tender mercies."

THE WORD MERCY IN ITS ORIGINAL HEBREW CARRIES THE CONNOTATION OF TENDERNESS.

The word *mercy* in its original Hebrew carries the connotation of *tenderness*. It speaks of the same manner of tenderness, love, and compassion as we would think of being used by a mother in picking up a son or daughter who had just been hit by a car.

How would a mom or a dad pick up a child that had just suffered such trauma? They would run to the child, drop to their knees, and with the most tender compassion and love, they would lift up that child to them. This is precisely what God's mercy does for us. When we've been hit on the road of life, God stoops down to where we are, and He tenderly lifts us to himself! Oh, such tender mercies! Oh, marvelous mercy!

Verse eight trumpets the fact that God is *full of mercy* and *abundant in the distribution of mercy.* Verse nine declares that God has been more than fair with you and me. Then the Psalmist exudes in verse 11, "For as the heaven is high above the earth, so great is his mercy toward them that fear him."

"For as the heaven is high above the earth"—the Hebrew for this phrase could properly be translated, *as great as the highest of heaven*—"So great is his mercy toward them that fear him." How tall is God's mercy? It is as great or as tall as the highest heaven.

You and I are limited in our reach according to our height. The taller we are, the longer our reach. How tall is God's mercy? How far can He reach? He can reach into the highest heaven. He can also stretch to lift a soul from the lowest gutter or abyss.

How tall is heaven above the earth? You and I can see the moon. It is an average distance of 238,900 miles high. That is quite a tall heaven, but it is only the beginning.

How high is the highest heaven? The sun is some 93,000,000 miles from earth. We humans behold its bright glow. That is incredibly high. Yet astronomers vouch that the sun is one of the closest of the universe's stars.

Heaven is monstrously higher than the sun. In fact, scientists inform us that the universe continues to expand at the speed of light. The sky is literally rising with each passing moment. Heaven just keeps on getting taller at the rate of 186,000 miles per second! Think of it! God's mercy toward us is as tall as the highest heaven!

Nature gives us a great lesson on mercy by the example of the way in which a mother eagle will train her eaglets to fly. First, mama eagle removes some of the cushioning from the nest. The cushioning served to make the baby eagles comfortable while in the nest. However, when it's time for the eaglets to become more mature and fly, the mother eagle removes

> **GOD'S MERCY TOWARD US IS AS TALL AS THE HIGHEST HEAVEN!**

some of the cushion. The nest is purposely made uncomfortable. It is a prelude to soaring. Were the nest to remain too cozy, the eaglets might be prone to become "couch potatoes."

After a time, the mother eagle will nudge her eaglets to the edge of the nest. If they cling there, she will even push them out of the nest.

Normally the eaglets' first attempts at flight are failures. They flap in desperation but not with finesse. Instead of flying, they fall. It sounds scary. It is scary when there is nothing below but large and jagged boulders.

There is good news, though, for a falling eaglet. Mother eagle can fly faster than an eaglet can fall! She swoops beneath an eaglet and catches it on her back and lifts it back to the nest. This process is repeated until the eaglet learns to take flight on its own. It isn't long, then, until it begins to soar.

The awesome truth is that God's marvelous mercy can fly faster than you and I can fall. Oh, the reach of the mercy of God! The Lord can stretch and reach so very far.

In verse 12 we are reassured, "As far as the east is from the west, so far hath he removed our transgressions from us." How far is the east from the west? How far?

One of the things a student learns early in geography is that if one goes north and keeps going that way long enough, they will eventually be headed south. The converse is also true. South, when pursued far enough, eventually turns into a northerly direction

However, this idea is not true of east and west. East and west never meet. When the Lord spoke of removing our transgressions from us, He purposely did not suggest that it is done in a northern or southern direction. He pointedly used the directions of east and west to make it clear that we would never have to worry about running into our old sins again somewhere on the road of life.

Notice again verse 13, "Like as a father pitieth his children, so the Lord pitieth them that fear him." Those of us who are parents or grandparents understand full well that our children can get to us. They are in our hearts. They even have a way of getting into our pocketbooks.

One of my granddaughters at age two requested on the phone that I would mail her some bubble gum. I went to the store. I bought the gum. I packaged it along with a note, and I mailed it. It cost more to mail the bubble gum than to purchase it. Incidentally, the night after Jade received the bubble gum in the mail, when she said her bedtime prayers, she prayed, "And Jesus, help my Papa Robert to mail me some bubble gum every day." Every grandparent has a similar story. We don't have to do these things, but we enjoy doing them because we love our grandchildren.

The same kind of feelings that we have for our children and grandchildren, God has even more intensely for you and me. We stand by our offspring when they go through hard times and do what we can to assist them. How much more is this true of our God! He does understand that we are human. He has promised to never leave us nor forsake us. The mercy of the Lord is from everlasting to everlasting upon them that fear Him. His Kingdom ruleth over all. As a dear preacher friend of mine often says, "Hell ain't in charge of nuthin'!"

His Hands

Mark 10:13-16 tells us much about our Savior's hands:

"And they brought young children to him, that he should touch them: and his disciples rebuked those that brought them.

But when Jesus saw it, he was much displeased, and said unto them, Suffer the little children to come unto me, and forbid them not: for of such is the kingdom of God.

Verily I say unto you, Whosoever shall not receive the kingdom of God as a little child, he shall not enter therein.

And he took them up in his arms, put his hands upon them, and blessed them."

Hands—what a marvelous bit of creation by the Master Genius of the universe! So often an individual's hands tell a story. If an attentive person studies the hands of another, providing they can read the evidence correctly, it often reveals much about the lifestyle and sometimes even the character of the person to whom the hands are attached.

It is no different with the hands of Jesus. His hands reveal to us so much about His person. They manifest His sturdy character and His ability to save us from ourselves, from the devil, and from the world.

Consider His Character

1 Peter 2:22 says,

"Who did no sin, neither was guile found in his mouth."

Don't hurry past the declaration that He *"did* no sin." [Emphasis added] Some of the main tools used for sinning are the human hands. With the hands, people steal. With the hands, humans deceive others. With the hands, mortals take the lives of other mortals. With the hands, men and women participate in immorality.

But His hands never participated in any vice. His hands were clean hands. His hands were undefiled and harmless. His hands were neither tainted nor stained with any evil.

Jesus Christ was a unique person with a sterling character. J. Oswald Sanders, in his terrific book, *The Incomparable Christ,* points out the uniqueness of Christ's character. I have summarized some of his thoughts below.

- No word that He spoke ever needed to be modified or withdrawn.
- He never needed to apologize for any word or action.
- He never had to confess failure to live up to the highest divine standards.
- He never asked for personal pardon, because He never needed to repent.
- He never sought or needed advice from the wisest men of His day.
- He never felt the need to justify ambiguous conduct, because His conscience was totally free from any condemnation.
- He never asked for prayer from others for himself.

It is no wonder that mothers wanted Jesus to place His hands on their children and pray for them. His hands belonged to a man of absolute moral perfection. His hands had the ability to minister to the deepest needs of human life.

A Closer Look at His Hands

Mark 6:3a asks,

"Is not this the carpenter?"

The only fragment we have of the biography of Jesus between ages 12 and 30 is wrapped up in these words—*the carpenter*. God chose to come to this world as a manual laborer. He, who could have chosen to be CEO of the world's largest corporation, chose to come as a carpenter. He made this choice to clearly and fully identify with the common people.

It has been observed that Jesus spent six times as long working at a carpenter's bench than He did in His public ministry. The normal workday during that period of time was 12 hours. They also had six-day workweeks. He worked steadily—12 hours per day, six days per week—for 18 years.

Jesus, no doubt, handled heavy lumber. Justin Martyr, who lived shortly after the apostles lived, informs us that Jesus used carpentry tools to make farm plows and yokes for oxen. He probably also made pieces of furniture. Yes, those were His hands at work.

While teaching one day, Jesus stated, "My yoke is easy." He knew a lot about yokes. He certainly knew how to make them. If a yoke were not constructed properly, it would chafe the neck of the oxen. An easy yoke was one that didn't agitate the neck of the animals.

Jesus tells all would-be disciples that His yoke is easy. In other words, it won't agitate you as you go through life. You won't chafe under His yoke. The reason is that He made this yoke with His own hands.

His hands were strong hands. His hands were developed by years of manual labor in a carpenter's shop. His hands were muscular and had a powerful grip. His hands can perform any task that you need done in your life.

At Calvary, they crucified Jesus. They put a sturdy nail through the palms of each of His hands. His hands, which were so pure and clean and strong, now bear a disfiguration. His hands are now nail-scarred.

After His resurrection, Jesus appeared to His disciples. He looked deep into the eyes and heart of doubting Thomas and said, "Behold my hands."

I offer you Jesus. Behold His hands. He has a long reach!

His hands can heal your body. More importantly, Jesus can forgive your sins, and He can save your soul.

The contemporary songwriter, Randy Phillips, put the message like this.

"No one can touch you like Jesus can,
No one can give you peace you cannot understand,
No one can bind your wounds with nail-scarred hands,
No one can touch you like Jesus can."

Marvelous mercy!

CHAPTER FOURTEEN

One Gift That God Values Above Sacrifice

In Hosea 6:6, we learn:

"For I desired mercy, and not sacrifice; and the knowledge of God more than burnt offerings."

This brief verse of scripture gives some of the most enlightening insights into the heart and mind of God that can be found anywhere in the entirety of the Old Testament. This Word from God, through the prophet Hosea, is profound. It is truly a revelation. The truth of this one Bible verse has far-reaching implications for our spiritual and natural lives.

This one scripture has enough force packed into it to change the very face and focus of religion. The concepts presented here, if adopted, can literally revolutionize a person's relationship and walk with God.

God intended, when He spoke these poignant words, to change the way people think and the way people live. This is high-potency truth.

Notice again, carefully, the introductory language of this verse, "For I desired." This is Almighty God speaking. He is in the process of expressing what it is that He really wants out of human beings. His prescription for humanity is in two parts.

Since the focus of this chapter will be on the first part of this divinely inspired prescription, I will take a moment before plunging into that subject to speak of the second part of this divine wish list.

"For I desired... the knowledge of God more than burnt offerings." The Lord is making a bold declaration that there is something He values far above animal sacrifices.

Pause for a moment. Be reminded that it was the Lord, through His servant Moses, who instituted animal sacrifices as a part of religious worship and service. But here and now, in Hosea 6:6, God is affirming that the sacrifice of animals is not the ultimate goal, neither of personal devotions, nor of corporate worship. The Almighty flatly states that what He is really wanting is that we human beings would come to "the knowledge of God!"

The Lord doesn't wish for us to just know *about* Him. He desires, even longs, that we come to truly *know* Him. The inherent idea here is that of a relationship. God deeply desires that you and I and others come into a deep and abiding relationship with Him!

Now let us consider the first half of this divine prescription.

Mercy Is Above Sacrifice

"For I desired mercy, and not sacrifice." This is an eternal verity! We often hear the word *sacrifice* used in relation to our worship of and service to God. We have a tendency to think that sacrifice is the ultimate expression of love for God. According to Hosea 6:6, such an idea is not accurate.

There is one gift that God values above personal sacrifices made for Him. It is the gift of mercy. God wishes human beings to be compassionate and merciful.

This leads us to an important question—to whom is the gift of mercy to be given? To God? Nonsense! God does not need any mercy from us. He is never in a position that He

THERE IS ONE GIFT THAT GOD VALUES ABOVE PERSONAL SACRIFICES MADE FOR HIM. IT IS THE GIFT OF MERCY.

needs any mercy from anybody. You and I are incapable of granting any mercy to the Almighty. It is as absurd a thought as that of a small ant offering a large man a ride on its back. Again, God needs no mercy from us.

So for whom is the mercy given? Where, or to whom, is mercy to be granted and distributed? There is only one answer that makes any sense. God is speaking about our having *mercy upon our fellow human beings!*

Take a moment and get a hold of this. God is vouching that He would rather we had mercy on a deficient neighbor or brother or sister than for us to bring a sacrifice or gift to Him Who is perfect! Wow! I can hardly take all that into my brain.

Jesus Used this Verse in His Earthly Ministry

On at least two occasions, Jesus used this Old Testament scripture. Both times it was spoken as an admonishment to the Pharisees. He told them that they needed to go and *learn what this means*, "I will have mercy, and not sacrifice."

Matthew 12:1-7 is one such occasion:

> *"At that time Jesus went on the sabbath day through the corn; and his disciples were an hungred, and began to pluck the ears of corn, and to eat.*

> But when the Pharisees saw it, they said unto him, Behold, thy disciples do that which is not lawful to do upon the sabbath day.

> But he said unto them, Have ye not read what David did, when he was an hungred, and they that were with him;

> How he entered into the house of God, and did eat the shewbread, which was not lawful for him to eat, neither for them which were with him, but only for the priests?

> Or have ye not read in the law, how that on the sabbath days the priests in the temple profane the sabbath, and are blameless?

> But I say unto you, That in this place is one greater than the temple.

> But if ye had known what this meaneth, I will have mercy, and not sacrifice, ye would not have condemned the guiltless."

The disciples were plucking (harvesting, working) grain. The Pharisees noted to Jesus that this was unlawful. Jesus introduces here *the doctrine of human necessity.*

He used an Old Testament illustration of David and his men. They were famished and on the run for their lives. The priest on duty gave them shewbread to eat from the Holy Place in the Tabernacle. Normally, this would not be done. In fact, under normal conditions such actions were totally unacceptable. However, Jesus notes that under the prevailing dire circumstances, it was a humane and acceptable remedy.

Jesus then used a contemporary example. He referred to the priests who served (worked) weekly in the Temple on the Sabbath day; thus, they actually violated the Mosaic Law. The force of this teaching by Jesus is not an attempt to encourage persons to work on the Lord's Day. What Jesus is defining is that when it comes to evaluating the actions of our fellow human beings, we must consider two primary matters: circumstances and motives, which are deduced from their circumstances and actions.

He then affirmed that if the Pharisees truly understood the principle of Hosea 6:6, they "would not have condemned the guiltless." Moffatt translates the phrase this way, "you would not have condemned men who are not guilty." This was a direct reference to the disciples and their actions of plucking and eating grain. The NCV translates the statement like this, "you would not judge those who have done nothing wrong." This is a most interesting doctrine and worth additional time of reflection.

> LET US GIVE TO OUR NEIGHBORS AND THE WORLD THE ONE GIFT THAT GOD VALUES ABOVE SACRIFICE — MERCY.

The other time Jesus used this Old Testament scripture and principle is recorded in Matthew 9:10-13.

> *"And it came to pass, as Jesus sat at meat in the house, behold, many publicans and sinners came and sat down with him and his disciples.*
>
> *And when the Pharisees saw it, they said unto his disciples, Why eateth your Master with publicans and sinners?*
>
> *But when Jesus heard that, he said unto them, They that be whole need not a physician, but they that are sick.*
>
> *But go ye and learn what that meaneth, I will have mercy, and not sacrifice: for I am not come to call the righteous, but sinners to repentance."*

Jesus was eating (associating, fellowshipping) with sinners. The Pharisees were critical of this behavior of Jesus. They considered themselves too holy to fellowship with sinners. Jesus articulated that it is the spiritually ill (sinners) who need a loving, helping, and healing hand. He further postulated that God would rather that we would help a sinner—have mercy on him or her—than bring a gift or sacrifice for God. There is a gift that God values above sacrifice. It is the gift of mercy bestowed on a fellow human being.

Practical Application

We need to rid ourselves of all the following:

- Animosity and malice;
- Resentment and bitterness;
- Gossip and backbiting;
- Unforgiveness and revenge;
- Harshness and judgmental attitudes;
- Grudges and harbored ill will;
- Jealousies and envying;
- Emulations and egomania competitions; and,
- Strife and fighting.

We need to ask God to baptize us—to immerse us—in:

- Love and compassion;
- Mercy and forgiveness;
- Charity and benevolence;
- Humility and patience; and,
- Generosity and willingness.

What kind of person would you be if you truly understood and behaved according to this principle and truth? What kind of churches would we offer to wrecked humanity? What kind of communities and nation would we become? What kind of world would this be?

One Gift that God Values Above Sacrifice

Let us give to our neighbors and the world the one gift that God values above sacrifice—mercy. Only then does Jesus truly become the Lord of all the kingdoms of our hearts.

Why not begin by forgiving someone right now?

Mercy!

CHAPTER FIFTEEN

The Place Where Death Stopped

In 2 Samuel 24:15-16; 25, we read:

> "So the LORD sent a pestilence upon Israel from the morning even to the time appointed: and there died of the people from Dan even to Beer-sheba seventy thousand men.

> And when the angel stretched out his hand upon Jerusalem to destroy it, the LORD repented him of the evil, and said to the angel that destroyed the people, It is enough: stay now thine hand. And the angel of the LORD was by the threshingplace of Araunah the Jebusite."

> "And David built there an altar unto the LORD, and offered burnt offerings and peace offerings. So the LORD was intreated for the land, and the plague was stayed from Israel."

In our biblical story, the Lord God was extremely agitated with the spiritual fickleness of the Israelites. At the very same time, their leader, King David, also made a grave mistake in kingly judgment.

The end result of this combination of failures was that God directed a plague against Israel to punish them for their sins and to bring
them to repentance.

During the three days that this pestilence was upon the
land, some 70,000 people died. Imagine the impact on that
tiny nation.

On September 11, 2001, more than 3,000 individuals died in
a series of terrorist attacks upon the United States of America.
America was in shock! To understand the impact of the calamity
recorded in 2 Samuel 24 on the much tinier nation of Israel, mul-
tiply the death toll that resulted from the infamous September 11th
attack by 23, and you will begin to understand the magnitude of
this plague upon the Israelites.

In the biblical event, the death angel had gone throughout the
land. He then approached Jerusalem for a final assault. At this
point, the Lord gave the order to halt the grievous plague.

David became aware that the death angel was paused near
the city. King David literally saw the angel of death. It was standing near the threshing place, or barn, of the Jebusite king, a
farmer named Araunah.

King David was instructed by a prophet named Gad to build
an altar unto the Lord in the very location where the death angel
had stood as a sentinel. Upon that altar, David offered sacrifices
unto God. The Word of God declares that the Lord accepted the
sacrifices of David. The pestilence was terminated and wreaked
no more havoc on Israel.

That small area of ground where the sacrifices were made and
the death angel ceased to mete out judgment became memorial-
ized in the land of Palestine. That plot of ground became known
as *the place where death stopped.*

Another Miracle at that Same Location

Genesis 22:1-3; 6-14 states:

"And it came to pass after these things, that God did tempt Abraham, and said unto him, Abraham: and he said, Behold, here I am.

And he said, Take now thy son, thine only son Isaac, whom thou lovest, and get thee into the land of Moriah; and offer him there for a burnt offering upon one of the mountains which I will tell thee of.

And Abraham rose up early in the morning, and saddled his ass, and took two of his young men with him, and Isaac his son, and clave the wood for the burnt offering, and rose up, and went unto the place of which God had told him."

"And Abraham took the wood of the burnt offering, and laid it upon Isaac his son; and he took the fire in his hand, and a knife; and they went both of them together.

And Isaac spake unto Abraham his father, and said, My father: and he said, Here am I, my son. And he said, Behold the fire and the wood: but where is the lamb for a burnt offering?

And Abraham said, My son, God will provide himself a lamb for a burnt offering: so they went both of them together.

And they came to the place which God had told him of; and Abraham built an altar there, and laid the wood in order, and bound Isaac his son, and laid him on the altar upon the wood.

And Abraham stretched forth his hand, and took the knife to slay his son.

And the angel of the LORD called unto him out of heaven, and said, Abraham, Abraham: and he said, Here am I.

And he said, Lay not thine hand upon the lad, neither do thou any thing unto him: for now I know that thou fearest God, seeing thou hast not withheld thy son, thine only son from me.

And Abraham lifted up his eyes, and looked, and behold behind him a ram caught in a thicket by his horns: and Abraham went and took the ram, and offered him up for a burnt offering in the stead of his son.

And Abraham called the name of that place Jehovah-jireh: as it is said to this day, In the mount of the LORD it shall be seen."

This incident took place at the same location that later would be the site of the appearance of the death angel and the construction of an altar by King David near the barn of Araunah the Jebusite. The episode involving Abraham and Isaac occurred some 855 years prior to that later event.

ABRAHAM NAMED THE LOCATION JEHOVAHJIREH, WHICH MEANS THE LORD THAT PROVIDES.

Abraham thought that he was going to have to sacrifice his son, Isaac. God miraculously provided a ram as a substitute for Isaac. Abraham named the location *Jehovah-jireh*, which means *the Lord that provides*.

Isaac was spared from death on the very plot of ground that would later be owned by Araunah the Jebusite. Whenever

Abraham and Isaac viewed that hillside, they always had a special reverence for that place. It certainly was for them *the place where death stopped*.

Yet Another Miracle at that Same Location

John 19:16-20; 30; 40-42 tells us:

> *"Then delivered he him therefore unto them to be crucified. And they took Jesus, and led him away.*
>
> *And he bearing his cross went forth into a place called the place of a skull, which is called in the Hebrew Golgotha:*
>
> *Where they crucified him, and two other with him, on either side one, and Jesus in the midst.*
>
> *And Pilate wrote a title, and put it on the cross. And the writing was, JESUS OF NAZARETH THE KING OF THE JEWS.*
>
> *This title then read many of the Jews:* **for the place where Jesus was crucified was nigh to the city:** *and it was written in Hebrew, and Greek, and Latin."* [Emphasis added]
>
> *"When Jesus therefore had received the vinegar, he said, It is finished: and he bowed his head, and gave up the ghost."*
>
> *"Then took they the body of Jesus, and wound it in linen clothes with the spices, as the manner of the Jews is to bury.*
>
> *Now in the place where he was crucified there was a garden; and in the garden a new sepulchre, wherein was never man yet laid.*

There laid they Jesus therefore because of the
Jews' preparation day; for the sepulchre was nigh
at hand."

Luke 24:1-6a tells us more of the story:

"Now upon the first day of the week, very early in the
morning, they came unto the sepulchre, bringing the
spices which they had prepared, and certain others
with them.

And they found the stone rolled away from the
sepulchre.

And they entered in, and found not the body of the
Lord Jesus.

And it came to pass, as they were much perplexed
thereabout, behold, two men stood by them in shining
garments:

And as they were afraid, and bowed down their faces to
the earth, they said unto them, Why seek ye the living
among the dead?

He is not here, but is risen."

It is simply amazing. One thousand and fifty-one years after
the episode of King David and the death angel, Jesus Christ was
crucified at that same location near the city of Jerusalem. Not only did Jesus die there, He was also buried there.

JESUS RESURRECTED. HE LITERALLY WALKED OUT OF THAT TOMB, SECURELY GRASPING IN HIS HANDS THE KEYS OF DEATH, HELL, AND THE GRAVE.

Then, on that first Easter morning nearly 2,000 years ago, Jesus resurrected.

He literally walked out of that tomb, securely grasping in His hands the keys of death, hell, and the grave. That plot of ground again became *the place where death stopped!*

Jesus declared a wonderful promise and glorious truth in John 14:19:

> *"Yet a little while, and the world seeth me no more;*
> *but ye see me:* **because I live, ye shall live also.***"*
> [Emphasis added]

To put our faith in Christ and to obey the gospel means that for us also that plot of ground on which Jesus was crucified and where He arose from the dead is *the place where death stopped.* Jesus did not die in vain.

Perhaps the following illustration from history will help us better understand what Christ's death and resurrection have truly provided for each of us.

The Roman Coliseum had become a center for government-sponsored entertainment, which had become exceedingly barbaric. The live entertainment provided included gladiator fights. These were bloody, brutal, and gory.

As this travesty of human sacrifice for sport continued in Rome, far to the south in Italy there was a young man who was studying and preparing for the ministry. He was completely unaware of the cruelty and killing for entertainment that was taking place in Rome.

There came a time when this young, aspiring minister made a trip to the big city. In Rome, he noticed thousands of people pouring into the Coliseum. It was an amazing structure, so he decided to follow them and to check out what was happening there.

The young preacher was aghast at the violence on display. He watched the intense gladiator competition until the apparent loser lay helplessly upon the ground. The winner stood over the loser with his foot firmly planted on his opponent's neck. The young man in the stands suddenly realized that the defeated man was about to have his life taken. All this while the crowd looked on approvingly.

The horrified young man stood and in panicky desperation began to run down the sloping aisle toward the center of the arena. As he ran, he screamed as loud as he could, "Stop! Stop! In the name of God, stop!"

The Coliseum hushed into silence and all eyes focused on the young man. He rushed across the open arena and flung himself across the body of the collapsed gladiator. It was a stunning display of compassion in an arena and a society filled with violence and insensitivity.

The conquering gladiator hesitated only a moment and then coldly killed them both. The crowd watched in stunning disbelief. Silence and stillness hung heavy over the amphitheater. Someone had sacrificed himself attempting to save a helpless and doomed individual. The crowd just couldn't fathom that kind of selfless love.

Almost immediately, as the crowd sat in hushed silence, the victor began to feel uncomfortable. Somewhere up in the arena one man got up and headed for the exit. Another person quickly followed him. Soon it was hundreds and then thousands quietly moving toward the exit until the entire Coliseum was vacated. Only the two dead bodies remained on the turf below. The young preacher's body was still draped across the losing gladiator's body.

However, as the story is told, the young ministry student did not die in vain. His heartfelt and impulsive act that day is noted in history as the place and the time where gladiatorial contests stopped in Rome. It was the place where death stopped.

The Place Where Death Stopped

On a hill outside of Jerusalem, Jesus did the same thing for all humanity. He gave His life to stop death. Those who put their trust in Him, in an eternal sense, shall never die.

O, marvelous mercy!

CHAPTER SIXTEEN

Jesus Specializes in Hope

Psalm 119:49 (NIV) says,

> *"Remember your word to your servant, for you have given me hope."*

A quick review of Bible characters reminds us that several of them were known for one outstanding virtue. Here is a list of just a few Bible personalities with their notable traits.

- Noah—perseverance
- Job—patience
- Abraham—faith
- Moses—meekness
- Samuel—integrity
- David—worship
- Solomon—wisdom
- Daniel—devotion
- Paul—evangelism

However, Jesus is the only one of these that excels in every virtue. If, though, I had to select one trait about Him that means the most to humanity, my choice would be that *Jesus specializes in proffered hope*.

Dear reader, where would you be just now were it not for the hope that Christ has brought to your life? Jesus has given you hope when some aspects of your life looked completely hopeless. Jesus held out hope to you when perhaps others simply wrote you off as a failure. It is a blessed truth—Jesus specializes in hope.

A Better Future

Look again at the inspired record of John 1:1-4; 9-12:

> *"In the beginning was the Word, and the Word was with God, and the Word was God.*
>
> *The same was in the beginning with God.*
>
> *All things were made by him; and without him was not any thing made that was made.*
>
> *In him was life; and the life was the light of men."*
>
> *"That was the true Light, which lighteth every man that cometh into the world.*
>
> *He was in the world, and the world was made by him, and the world knew him not.*
>
> *He came unto his own, and his own received him not.*
>
> *But as many as received him, to them gave he power to become the sons of God, even to them that believe on his name."*

When Jesus came to earth, many of his own people did not receive Him. Regardless, to those who did welcome Him, He gave hope and power to become something that was never before possible—sons of God.

One time I received a letter written by a backslidden Christian. He was just beginning to turn his life around and get right with God again. In the letter he commented that God was increasing every little effort that he was putting forth toward the Lord. He was astounded that God would be so merciful to a backslider. It should not surprise us, for Jesus is merciful, and He specializes in hope.

Remember the sinful woman who was brought to Jesus in John 8? Religious fanatics who had no real concern for her brought her to Christ. They saw her only as an object to be manipulated for their hypocritical plotting.

Jesus assertively confronted the accusers. Silently and one by one, they eased away from the scene until the entire group of them had dispersed. Jesus spoke briefly with the woman and then sent her on her way with fresh hope conveyed by these parting words recorded in John 8:11b (NIV):

> "Then neither do I condemn you," Jesus declared. "**Go now and leave your life of sin.**" [Emphasis added]

The group, which had brought this woman to Jesus, were specialists in accusation and condemnation. Jesus stood out in contrast to them as a diamond does against a black cloth. He brilliantly shone that day as a beacon of hope. To that fallen woman, He was as a lighthouse, casting His welcoming light to a desperate soul on a storm-tossed sea. He offered her hope.

The Word of God makes a fearful and a wonderful assertion about these matters in James 2:12-13. Moffatt's translation puts it this way:

> "One alone is the legislator, who passes sentence; it is He who is able to save and to destroy; who are you, to judge your neighbor?
>
> for the judgment will be merciless to the man who has shown no mercy—whereas the merciful life will triumph in the face of judgment."

Weymouth translates the last phrase of verse 13 like this, "but mercy will triumph over judgment."

Still today, Jesus specializes in hope. A good question for you and me to answer is—In what do you and I specialize? Are we specialists in scorn, suspicion, accusation, and condemnation? Or, do we also specialize in giving people hope? It is true that we are to hate sin; it is also true that we are to love the sinner. It is my firm conviction that, especially for those of us in the ministry, one of our most important assignments is to offer individuals hope.

Jesus Is the Lifter

In Psalm 3:1-4, we read:

> *"LORD, how are they increased that trouble me! many are they that rise up against me.*
>
> *Many there be which say of my soul, There is no help for him in God. Selah.*
>
> *But thou, O LORD, art a shield for me; my glory, and the lifter up of mine head.*
>
> *I cried unto the LORD with my voice, and he heard me out of his holy hill. Selah."*

There are some 700 direct titles for God in the Scriptures. There are another 600 plus implied titles. Among the implied titles, *the Lifter* is a favorite of mine.

THERE ARE SOME 700 DIRECT TITLES FOR GOD IN THE SCRIPTURES.

The title *the Lifter* so succinctly, and yet so gloriously, describes the purpose and ministry of the Lord Jesus Christ! Jesus Christ is the Lifter! Consider the following scriptures and truths.

Deuteronomy 22:4 says,

> *"Thou shalt not see thy brother's ass or his ox fall down by the way, and hide thyself from them: thou shalt surely help him to **lift them up again**."* [Emphasis added]

This pointedly reveals the attitude and compassion of Almighty God—even toward a lowly animal. If God cares that much for a donkey, how much more does He care for you and me! This fact of love and mercy is clearly seen in the following teaching and action of Jesus, recorded in Matthew 12:10-13.

> *"And, behold, there was a man which had his hand withered. And they asked him, saying, Is it lawful to heal on the sabbath days? That they might accuse him.*
>
> *And he said unto them, What man shall there be among you, that shall have one sheep, and if it fall into a pit on the sabbath day, will he not lay hold on it, and lift it out?*
>
> *How much then is a man better than a sheep? Wherefore it is lawful to do well on the sabbath days.*
>
> *Then saith he to the man, Stretch forth thine hand. And he stretched it forth; and it was restored whole, like as the other."*

Jesus is the Lifter.

The Lift of Healing

Jesus used healing to lift individuals. Observe this episode in Luke 13:11-13:

> *"And, behold, there was a woman which had a spirit of infirmity eighteen years, and was bowed together, and could in no wise lift up herself.*

143

And when Jesus saw her, he called her to him, and said unto her, Woman, thou art loosed from thine infirmity.

And he laid his hands on her: and immediately she was made straight, and glorified God."

The vivid truth is that you and I can be *loosed* from whatever is holding us down.. That can be physical infirmity, or it can be from other problems including social, financial, personal, or spiritual disorders. Jesus is *the Lifter!*

THE VIVID TRUTH IS THAT YOU AND I CAN BE *LOOSED* FROM WHATEVER IS HOLDING US DOWN.

Here is further testimony from the Scriptures that affirms that our God is the Lifter.

Isaiah 59:19-20 says:

"So shall they fear the name of the LORD from the west, and his glory from the rising of the sun. When the enemy shall come in like a flood, the Spirit of the LORD shall lift up a standard against him.

And the Redeemer shall come to Zion, and unto them that turn from transgression in Jacob, saith the LORD."

Psalm 91:14-16 states:

"Because he hath set his love upon me, therefore will I deliver him: I will set him on high, because he hath known my name.

He shall call upon me, and I will answer him: I will be with him in trouble; I will deliver him, and honour him.

With long life will I satisfy him, and shew him my salvation."

Now notice Genesis 7:17 (NIV):

"For forty days the flood kept coming on the earth, and as the waters increased they lifted the ark high above the earth."

It is worth observing in the story of Noah and the Flood that the same waters that carried away and drowned the wicked also lifted up the ark and transported it safely.

Isaiah 64:8 says,

"But now, O LORD, thou art our father; we are the clay, and thou our potter; and we all are the work of thy hand."

What a great analogy the above verse is of God's working in the lives of His children. Have you ever paused and considered when a potter is working with clay to make a vessel, what the primary direction of his hands upon the clay is? The answer is **THE POTTER PRIMARILY PULLS UPWARD ON THE CLAY AS HE SHAPES FOR A USEFUL PURPOSE.** *upward.* The potter primarily pulls upward on the clay as he shapes for a useful purpose. Yes, our God is the Lifter.

A further encouragement along this same line is found in James 4:10, which says,

"Humble yourselves in the sight of the Lord, and he shall lift you up."

My friend, please don't ever forget this truth—Jesus is the Lifter.

We Rejoice in Hope

There are not many things in this world that can produce such intense rejoicing in the human heart like bona fide hope. The following passages speak of this truth.

Romans 5:1-2; 5 says:

> "Therefore being justified by faith, we have peace with God through our Lord Jesus Christ:
>
> By whom also we have access by faith into this grace wherein we stand, and rejoice in hope of the glory of God."
>
> "And hope maketh not ashamed; because the love of God is shed abroad in our hearts by the Holy Ghost which is given unto us."

In Titus 1:2, we read,

> "In hope of eternal life, which God, that cannot lie, promised before the world began."

Titus 2:11-14 states:

> "For the grace of God that bringeth salvation hath appeared to all men,
>
> Teaching us that, denying ungodliness and worldly lusts, we should live soberly, righteously, and godly, in this present world;
>
> Looking for that blessed hope, and the glorious appearing of the great God and our Saviour Jesus Christ;
>
> Who gave himself for us, that he might redeem us from all iniquity, and purify unto himself a peculiar people, zealous of good works."

Mary Magdalene

Mary Magdalene had apparently been a woman of the streets with a life full of sin. Jesus cast seven devils out of her and she was changed. Jesus lifted her and gave her hope, and Mary became a great disciple of the Christ.

Jesus Specializes in Hope

When Jesus resurrected from the dead, He appeared first to Mary Magdalene. After revealing His true identity to her, He sent her to the disciples with the message of His resurrection. The disciples refused to believe the report. Mark 16:9-11 gives this account:

> *"Now when Jesus was risen early the first day of the week, he appeared first to Mary Magdalene, out of whom he had cast seven devils.*
>
> *And she went and told them that had been with him, as they mourned and wept.*
>
> *And they, when they had heard that he was alive, and had been seen of her, believed not."*

Close examination of the biblical account informs us that part of their disbelief was the incredible assertion that a woman with her background had been the first to see Him alive again.

Why did Jesus choose Mary Magdalene for this distinguished honor? Why not Simon Peter, the man with the designated keys to the Kingdom? Why not James or John or Matthew? Why did he choose a loser who became a winner when Someone offered her hope?

I personally am convinced that Jesus purposefully gave this distinguished honor (of being the first to see Him after His resurrection) to Mary Magdalene. The Resurrection is all about *hope*. It is the hope of eternal life. It was another startling testimony that the gospel is all about lifting people, changing lives, and offering hope. Jesus specializes in hope.

O, what marvelous mercy!

CHAPTER SEVENTEEN

The Powerful Blood of Jesus Christ

1 Corinthians 6:19-20 teaches:

"What? know ye not that your body is the temple of the Holy Ghost which is in you, which ye have of God, and ye are not your own?

For ye are bought with a price: therefore glorify God in your body, and in your spirit, which are God's."

The TLB conveys the first portion of verse 20 in this manner:

"For God has bought you with a great price."

Along the same lines, 1 Peter 18-19 (NCV) says:

"You know that in the past you were living in a worthless way, a way passed down from the people who lived before you. But you were saved from that worthless life. You were bought, not with something that ruins like gold or silver,

but with the precious blood of Christ, who was a pure and perfect lamb."

149

The Word of God declares four irrefutable truths regarding the availability of personal salvation.

- Every believer has been *purchased* or *redeemed* at a cost;
- The price for redemption was exorbitant;
- The purchase price was paid with blood; and,
- That blood was not just any blood—it was the *precious blood* of the Lord Jesus Christ.

The Pre-requisite of Blood

It is an irrevocable biblical fact that the shedding of blood is a pre-requisite for forgiveness. Consider the force of the dictum recorded in Hebrews 9:22, which says,

> *"Indeed, under the law almost everything is purified with blood, and without the shedding of blood there is no forgiveness of sins."*

To understand this mandatory requirement, one must have a mental grasp of the reasons for such a drastic criterion. The root problem is *sin*. According to Romans 6:23, the penalty for sin is *death*.

> *"For the wages of sin is death; but the gift of God is eternal life through Jesus Christ our Lord."*

According to the Scriptures, the only acceptable payment for sin and the only way to avoid death is *blood*. The reason for this precept was given through Moses In Leviticus 17:11 (NIV):

> *"For the life of a creature is in the blood, and I have given it to you to make atonement for yourselves on the altar; it is the blood that makes atonement for one's life."*

The NASU puts it this way:

"For the life of the flesh is in the blood, and I have given it to you on the altar to make atonement for your souls; for it is the blood by reason of the life that makes atonement."

Spiritually, without the shedding of blood, there is none of the following:

- Purification or cleansing;
- Atonement; and,
- Remission or forgiveness.

The Blood of Jesus—A Superior Substance

The blood of Jesus is the only blood that permanently makes atonement for sin, as seen in Hebrews 10:1-4 (NIV)

"The law is only a shadow of the good things that are coming-not the realities themselves. For this reason it can never, by the same sacrifices repeated endlessly year after year, make perfect those who draw near to worship.

If it could, would they not have stopped being offered? For the worshipers would have been cleansed once for all, and would no longer have felt guilty for their sins.

But those sacrifices are an annual reminder of sins,

because it is impossible for the blood of bulls and goats to take away sins."

The very word *atonement* comes from the Hebrew word *kaphar*. One of its definitions is *to cover* (as with bitumen or pitch).

The plain truth is that the Old Testament sacrifices could not take away sins. The sins were not removed. They were simply covered and rolled ahead for one year. At the end of a year, an individual was not only guilty of the transgressions of that particular twelve months, but also of the accumulated sins for all the previous years.

The blood of Jesus is a superior substance. It doesn't just cover sins. It *removes, purges, and expunges* them! Notice this truth in Hebrews 10:5-6; 10-12a; 14-22 (NLT):

> *"That is why Christ, when he came into the world, said, 'You did not want animal sacrifices and grain offerings. But you have given me a body so that I may obey you.'*
>
> *No, you were not pleased with animals burned on the altar or with other offerings for sin."*
>
> *"And what God wants is for us to be made holy by the sacrifice of the body of Jesus Christ once for all time.*
>
> *Under the old covenant, the priest stands before the altar day after day, offering sacrifices that can never take away sins.*
>
> *But our High Priest offered himself to God as one sacrifice for sins, good for all time."*
>
> *"For by that one offering he perfected forever all those whom he is making holy.*
>
> *And the Holy Spirit also testifies that this is so. First he says,*
>
> *'This is the new covenant I will make with my people on that day, says the Lord: I will put my laws in their hearts so they will understand them, and I will write them on their minds so they will obey them.'*
>
> *Then he adds, 'I will never again remember their sins and lawless deeds.'*

Now when sins have been forgiven, there is no need to offer any more sacrifices.

And so, dear brothers and sisters, we can boldly enter heaven's Most Holy Place because of the blood of Jesus.

This is the new, life-giving way that Christ has opened up for us through the sacred curtain, by means of his death for us.

And since we have a great High Priest who rules over God's people,

Let us go right into the presence of God, with true hearts fully trusting him. For our evil consciences have been sprinkled with Christ's blood to make us clean, and our bodies have been washed with pure water."

The blood of Jesus is indeed a superior substance. Through it we obtain *marvelous mercy*.

Precious Blood

The Holy Scriptures' valuation of the blood of Jesus is that it is precious blood. One of the denotations of the word *precious* is *limited quantity*.

An illustration of this definition is gold. It is considered a precious metal. This is, in part, because there is only a limited quantity available. In fact, it is estimated that if all the gold that has ever been mined were heaped in one pile, it would only be one-third as tall as the Washington Monument.

Jesus, as a human adult, had only some five quarts of blood. The limited quantity is one of the reasons His blood is precious. The good news is that limited quantity was sufficient as a remedy for sin because it was inherently and intrinsically *pure*.

His blood was not only pure, it also remains *forever pure*. It is the only detergent that can produce 1,000 percent cleansing.

HIS BLOOD WAS NOT ONLY PURE, IT ALSO REMAINS FOREVER PURE. All other detergents and cleansers break down in time when brought into contact with uncleanness and contamination. The blood of Christ has flowed over many a filthy soul. Think of all the evil, the debauchery, and the wickedness that the Blood has washed away; yet, it remains as pure today as when it was first shed on Calvary. The songwriter penned it accurately, "The Blood will never lose its power."

The blood of Jesus is precious because it is *priceless*.

The Cross

It was not just a coincidence that the cross of Jesus had two arms. The Bible clearly teaches that those who were saved in the Old Testament looked *forward* to the saving work of Christ on the cross. Those who are being saved today look to the same saving work by looking *rearward* to His cross.

Thus, one arm of Christ on the cross was outstretched to cover all the Old Testament believers all the way back to Adam. The other extended arm of Jesus reached forward to cover all New Testament believers. The one death of Jesus covered all Old and New Testament era sins.

A Stupendous Promise

In Hebrews 8:12, God promises:

> *"For I will be merciful to their unrighteousness, and their sins and their iniquities will I remember no more."*

When God forgives and remits, He promises to never again remember the offending transgressions.

Let's compare and contrast this annihilation of our offenses with certain facets of the modern computer. The user of the computer can signal to delete data. A pop-up notice will usually inquire, "Are you sure you want to delete this file?" The user can then confirm the decision.

In comparison, on Calvary, Jesus signaled to delete our sins. It is up to you and me to confirm that decision in our personal lives. We do this through conversion by obeying the gospel of Jesus Christ.

In contrast, with a computer, the deleted information can later be retrieved. This can be accomplished by using the undo button, or by visiting the recycle bin, or by bringing out a previously copied back-up disk, or by the genius of a computer expert.

> CALVARY HAS NO UNDO BUTTON, JESUS KEEPS NO BACK-UP DISKS, AND CHRISTIANS ARE ENCOURAGED NOT TO DEVELOP A RECYCLE BIN.

Here's great news. Calvary has no undo button, Jesus keeps no back-up disks, and Christians are encouraged not to develop a recycle bin. O, marvelous mercy!

Pleading the Blood of Jesus

It is not uncommon around Spirit-filled churches to hear believers speaking about "pleading the blood of Jesus." I confess that for years I did not really understand the concept, though I saw obvious proof that, when used sincerely, it worked.

"I plead the blood of Jesus." These are not some magical words. They are part and parcel of an important biblical principle. This plea refers back to the truth that each authentic believer has been *purchased and redeemed* by the blood of Jesus. The Hebrew word for *plead* is *riyb*. One of its definitions is *to conduct legal proceedings*.

Jesus is the rightful owner of every child of God and all of which he or she dedicates to the Lord. It is totally appropriate to plead the blood of Jesus over personal items such as these:

- Life
- Marriage
- Family
- Home
- Employment
- Finances
- Ministry
- Future

When genuine disciples plead the blood of Jesus in the face of demonic forces, it is a plea of legal consequence in the spirit world. It is a stark and jolting reminder to any and every imp of hell that the devil has no legal claim of ownership with regard to that follower of Jesus. Satan is an imposter.

By pleading the blood of Jesus, a child of God is demanding that the devil vacate the premises. Satan cannot legally (or spiritually) remain on property where Jesus holds the title deed. Satan is forced to respect the ownership of Christ, back off, and exit.

The blood of Jesus Christ is, quite literally, the "flag" that flies over territory that is owned by the Savior. It establishes an enforceable boundary line that satan has no choice but to respect. "Pleading the Blood" brings God into the controversy.

The Bible reports that this is the weapon that followers of Christ will use to triumph over the devil. Notice carefully this prescription in Revelation 12:10-11a:

> "And I heard a loud voice saying in heaven, Now is come salvation, and strength, and the kingdom of our God, and the power of his Christ: for the accuser of our brethren is cast down, which accused them before our God day and night.

And they overcame him by the blood of the Lamb."

An Unmatched Weapon

Many of the weapons of the Christian and the Church have been counterfeited by satan or persons used by him. Consider the following list of opposing weapons:

- Holy Spirit vs. false spirits;
- Truth vs. lies;
- Prophets vs. false prophets; and,
- Messiah vs. Anti-Christ.

There is one weapon that satan has no counterfeit for, nor will he ever—the blood of Jesus Christ! You see, satan is a fallen angel. Angels have no blood. *If* satan did have blood, he would have to die to give it! He is not about to do that.

The powerful blood of Jesus is a weapon without any counter-defense. Satan can't defend against it. *It is the Church's and the Christian's nuclear bomb!* So, when the devil harasses you, "nuke" him. Drop a bomb on him—plead the blood of Jesus!

CHAPTER EIGHTEEN

The Affirming Witness of a Sheep

Psalm 23 is often called "The Shepherd's Psalm." The fact is, though, it is not the Shepherd talking. This is the affirming witness of a sheep and it is a testimony that resonates with worship.

"The LORD is my shepherd; I shall not want.

He maketh me to lie down in green pastures: he leadeth me beside the still waters.

He restoreth my soul: he leadeth me in the paths of righteousness for his name's sake.

Yea, though I walk through the valley of the shadow of death, I will fear no evil: for thou art with me; thy rod and thy staff they comfort me.

Thou preparest a table before me in the presence of mine enemies: thou anointest my head with oil; my cup runneth over.

Surely goodness and mercy shall follow me all the days of my life: and I will dwell in the house of the LORD forever."

The sheep declares, "The LORD is my shepherd, I shall not want." In current vernacular, the affirming witness of this sheep is, "I've got the Lord looking out for me." Wow! Certainly there is no better guardian or shepherd than the Lord God.

THE AFFIRMING WITNESS OF THIS SHEEP IS, "I'VE GOT THE LORD LOOKING OUT FOR ME."

"I shall not want." The reporting sheep is expressing a deep inner security because it recognizes that it is receiving the best of care from the Shepherd. The sheep has nothing about which to complain.

Is this not true with us as well? God's children live more kingly than kings. I am not referring to material wealth. I am speaking concerning the riches that money cannot buy, such as being the benefactors of marvelous mercy. As for me, I have not one complaint to lodge against the Lord.

The affirming witness of the sheep continues in verse 2. "He maketh me to lie down in green pastures." David, the writer of this psalm, was very familiar with the Judean hills. He was keenly aware that green pastures are not the norm in that area. The usual ground there is barren or quite stony. A shepherd that leads his flock to green pastures is either a knowledgeable one, or an aggressive one, or both. He must either know where the green pastures are or he must search for them. A good shepherd never leaves his sheep in the wilderness.

Sometimes as believers we have to walk through the wilderness and the rocky places, but God does not leave us there. He always brings us to a place of rest at just the right time.

The sheep continues his witness concerning the Shepherd, saying, "he leadeth me beside the still waters." The significance of still waters is that they are a safe area for drinking. It is here that the sheep are refreshed. Some waters move too swiftly for sheep. A strong current can endanger the lives of sheep. A good shepherd never unduly risks the lives of his sheep.

In our present society, Christians have to be extremely careful regarding the source from which we get our waters of refreshment. A lot of the "waters" of entertainment in today's world are fast-paced and replete with dangerous rapids and treacherous

CHRISTIANS HAVE TO BE EXTREMELY CAREFUL REGARDING THE SOURCE FROM WHICH WE GET OUR WATERS OF REFRESHMENT.

whirlpools. However, if we truly follow the Shepherd, He will always provide safe areas for our refreshing.

In verse 2, the psalmist mentions pastures and waters. Those have to do primarily with the physical needs of the body. The Shepherd indeed looks after our physical and material needs.

In verse 3, the sheep acknowledges, "He restoreth my soul." This is a reference to *inward needs*. The same Shepherd that provides for the requirements of our bodies also takes good care of our souls. Life has a way of wearing on us. Our bodies can get weary, but so can our minds and our very souls. Thankfully, the same Shepherd that puts a roof over our heads, clothes on our backs, and food on our tables, also knows how to refresh and restore the deepest part of our being.

Next, the sheep reports, "he leadeth me in the paths of righteousness for his name's sake." A superb shepherd is always careful with regard to the paths in which he leads his sheep. He selects good paths; often, they are familiar ones.

It is reported that in Bible times shepherds developed reputations for the way in which they took care of their sheep. If a shepherd was careless, he would let his sheep go through places that matted or tore their wool. When such a shepherd would take his sheep to the market, those who were buyers would examine these sheep thoroughly before possibly purchasing them.

By contrast, some shepherds had built such a reputation for proper care of their sheep that the buyers would purchase from them without even examining the sheep. Each shepherd had a reputation. His "name" or reputation was founded upon his handling of his sheep.

> EACH SHEPHERD HAD A REPUTATION. HIS "NAME" OR REPUTATION WAS FOUNDED UPON HIS HANDLING OF HIS SHEEP.

Don't overlook the fact that our Shepherd's name is on the line. His reputation is the best because of many reasons, including how He takes care of His sheep. David contended in Psalm 23 that the Shepherd led him in paths of righteousness because His name was on the line. He's got a reputation at stake! "He leads me in the paths of righteousness for his name's sake."

Verse 4 gives us this confident testimony from the sheep, "Yea, though I walk through the valley of the shadow of death, I will fear no evil: for thou art with me..." Over the years, I have heard and read several explanations for "the valley of the shadow of death." No doubt most or all of them have some validity.

One explanation that intrigues me reports that sometimes the sheep are led to new pastures along very narrow and winding paths high up on the hillsides. At times, these paths diminish until they are barely two feet wide. Often along such paths, there is a sheer drop-off of several hundred or even 1,000 feet. The valley below such treacherous paths is sometimes referred to as the valley of the shadow of death. Were a sheep to fall off one of those cliffs, it would be certain death.

A good shepherd is well aware of the threat such paths pose to his sheep. He also knows that the sheep tend to become fearful in such situations. So, in order to calm their fears and to keep them safely in line, he takes extra precautions while moving along such dangerous passageways.

One of the things that a concerned shepherd does under such circumstances is to talk to his sheep almost constantly. His confident voice reassures them that they can safely traverse this dangerous area. He gives them soothing words of encouragement. Then somewhere along the upward path, the shepherd will halt the forward movement. The shepherd will inch his way back down the complete line of the sheep until he reaches the very last one, all the while continuing to assuage any of their fears with his reassuring comments. Then he will slowly proceed back up the line, tapping each one gently with his staff and encouraging them that all is going to be well.

For all true believers, when in a scary or threatening place, there is nothing like hearing the voice of our Shepherd. Oh, the comfort that comes when in dire circumstances you suddenly recognize that the Shepherd is standing alongside you. Our Shepherd knows what He is doing and how to properly take care of you and me. You and I can make it safely with our Shepherd's assistance.

The sheep also notes in verse 4, "thy rod and thy staff they comfort me." The rod was a short stick about three feet long. Its primary purpose was to beat back predators and drive them away from the sheep. It was a weapon to be used in offense against the enemies of the sheep.

The staff, when upright, was usually the approximate height of the shepherd. It had a large crook on one end. The staff had several purposes. One major use for the staff was to help rescue a sheep that may have inadvertently slipped into a ditch or gotten entangled in some brush. The staff was a tool to be used in defense of the sheep.

The Lord our Shepherd has all the tools and weapons necessary to adequately take care of His sheep. What comfort is afforded to us through this understanding!

In verse 5, the sheep exults, "Thou preparest a table before me in the presence of mine enemies." For years, this phrase puzzled me. I just couldn't grasp the connection between a table and a sheep. The answer is that the table referred to here is not a kitchen table. In some contexts, it could refer to just a piece of leather or linen cloth spread upon the ground.

The word *table* as used here is an agricultural term. In this particular passage of scripture, its connotation has to do with a wounded sheep. Observe carefully the reference to, "in the presence of mine enemies." It is incredible, but apparently true, that other sheep show no grave concern for a wounded and bleeding member of the flock. Even as it lays motionless and unable to stand up, other sheep will eat all the grass right up to the wounded sheep. In fact, it is reported that sheep will even use their head to push a wounded sheep aside to eat the grass next to and under the fallen member of the flock.

A sensible shepherd knows that for a wounded sheep to recover it must eat. So, the shepherd stakes out an area of some 15 by 20 feet for the injured sheep. He places his rod at one end of said area and his staff at the other end. On one of the other borders, he will lay down his cloak. On the remaining border, he will place another object belonging to him or even lie down himself. All the sheep understand that no other sheep is allowed inside that table. It is reserved for the sheep that's hurting.

As Christians, we have a great Shepherd that takes care of us even when we are wounded. Our Shepherd doesn't give up on a sheep that is down. He prepares a "table" for us in the presence of our enemies. He makes sure that the supply that we need to fully recover is available to us.

OUR SHEPHERD DOESN'T GIVE UP ON A SHEEP THAT IS DOWN.

In the same verse, the sheep adds another important insight about the Shepherd, "thou anointest my head with oil." The word *anointing* is key to a proper understanding of this passage. One of its root meanings in Hebrew is *to smear upon or to rub in.* Shepherds would smear oil on the foreheads of the sheep and then massage it into the skin.

Shepherds anointed the heads of their sheep for several reasons. One of the obvious reasons has to do with the fact that it gets blistering hot in the arid and semi-desert land of Palestine. Anointing the sheep with olive oil had a cooling effect on the sheep.

Shepherds would also pour oil into the wounds of an injured sheep. This was to cleanse the wound and to aid in the healing. The oil had medicinal value.

We, the disciples of Jesus, sometimes just need to cool down. Other times, we need to heal. Our Shepherd helps us with both of these matters. His anointing is poured on us not only for our personal benefit, but also to bless others through us.

In verse 5, the sheep credits the Shepherd because, saying, "my cup runneth over." Particularly to the western mind, this is a phrase that needs some explanation. What is the connection between a sheep and a cup? The reference here is not a reference to a cup from the kitchen, such as we humans would use for a drink. The term *cup* as used here once again has an agricultural meaning.

A cup was a hollowed out piece of stone that usually was placed next to a well or a spring. Normally it was some two and one-half feet long, perhaps one and one-half feet wide and about a foot and one-half deep. Basically, it's what we now call a trough. In Old Testament Bible times, it was called a cup.

Such a cup was where the sheep would drink if the flock were not near a stream. The shepherd would draw water out of the well and fill the cup. Since the cup was carved out of stone and exposed to the blazing sun of that arid land, the cup itself would become very hot. Consequently, the water placed in the cup would soon be too warm to be desirable for drinking. So a good shepherd not only fills the cup, he keeps on pouring in fresh water and overflowing the cup as a method of cooling down the cup. After a while, the water in the cup is much more palatable and satisfying to the sheep.

What the psalmist is expressing is, "My shepherd takes care of me. He makes sure that the waters are not only sufficient, but also cool enough for me to drink and to enjoy!"

For the followers of Jesus, our Shepherd also gives us an abundant supply of exactly what we need. He knows what is appropriate for our well-being and enjoyment. We can say along with the psalmist, "my cup runneth over."

In verse 6, the sheep concludes its testimony with two bold and extremely positive statements. The sheep says first, "Surely goodness and mercy shall follow me all the days of my life." The sheep is affirming that it is convinced that the Shepherd, who has taken such excellent care of it up till now, will provide that same premium quality care for the rest of the sheep's life. There will be no let down. The Shepherd will continue to lead the sheep onward with that same compassionate care, bountiful provision, and watchful protection. Not only that, the Shepherd will also make sure that the sheep has a rearward guard. However, in this case it will not be a pedigreed sheepdog. It will be *goodness* and *mercy*. Think of it, folks—the blessing of being trailed the rest of life's journey by God's goodness and God's mercy!

The second and final forceful statement that concludes this magnificent Psalm is this, "and I will dwell in the house of the LORD for ever." To get a proper understanding of the significance of this statement, one must remember that sheep were usually kept outside under the shade of the trees and the stars of the night. However, once in a while a shepherd would "adopt" a sheep. He would bring the sheep into his tent and make it a family pet. In Psalm 23, this sheep is exulting that it will be a pet forever in the

Shepherd's house. It is not just going to be in the field, but the Shepherd is going to adopt it, take it into His house, and make it one of His pets!

To think that God would not only let you and me be in the sheepfold, but that He would actually bring us into His house is amazing. He feeds us with His food, makes us a part of His family, and honors us as one of His pets!

God is going to let me live in His house *forever*. This is goodness and mercy at their best!

CHAPTER NINETEEN

The Lord Gives More than We Request

Ephesians 3:17-21 states:

> *"That Christ may dwell in your hearts by faith; that ye, being rooted and grounded in love,*
>
> *May be able to comprehend with all saints what is the breadth, and length, and depth, and height;*
>
> *And to know the love of Christ, which passeth knowledge, that ye might be filled with all the fulness of God.*
>
> *Now unto him that is able to do exceeding abundantly above all that we ask or think, according to the power that worketh in us,*
>
> *Unto him be glory in the church by Christ Jesus throughout all ages, world without end. Amen."*

The triumphant revelation with reference to God in verse 20 is that *He is able!* God *is* able. It is not that God used to be able or that someday God will be able. God lives in the eternal present;

169

consequently, it can truthfully be stated of God at any and all times that He is able.

He is able to do all that you and I *ask*. Wonderfully, He can do above and beyond anything and everything that we dare to ask. Our asking will never render God's ability deficient nor exhaust His supply.

Sometimes we think of a prayer request, but for one reason or another we don't get around to asking God for it out loud. The glorious truth is that God is able to do all that we *think*. Here again, He can outperform our thinking. He can work above and beyond even our grandest thoughts.

To rivet this magnanimous concept of God into the hearts and faith of his readers, Paul adds the words "exceeding abundantly." The full description is "exceeding abundantly above all." The Greek words translated *exceeding abundantly* literally mean *superabundant, excessive, beyond measure*.

Reflect on that. God is able to do superabundantly above all that we ask. He can supercede, or do in excess of, all that we can think. God's ability is beyond measure and is indeed limitless.

GOD'S ABILITY IS BEYOND MEASURE AND IS INDEED LIMITLESS.

Some years ago a friend shared a paper that contained the following reading. It had no title. I have sought unsuccessfully to identify its author (I would be most happy to identify him or her in future editions of this book).

His goal is a relationship with *me*!

He will never leave me,

Never forsake me,

Never mislead me,

Never forget me,

The Lord Gives More than We Request

Never overlook me, and,

Never cancel my appointment in His appointment book!

———•◦•———

When I fall, He lifts me up!

When I fail, He forgives!

When I am weak, He is strong!

When I am lost, He is the way!

When I am afraid, He is my courage!

When I stumble, He steadies me!

When I am hurt, He heals me!

When I am broken, He mends me!

When I am blind, He leads me!

When I am hungry, He feeds me!

When I face trials, He is with me!

When I face persecution, He shields me!

When I face problems, He comforts me!

When I face loss, He provides for me!

When I face Death, He carries me Home!

———•◦•———

He is everything for everybody, everywhere,

Every time, and every way.

He is God, He is faithful.

I am His, and He is mine!

My Father in Heaven can whip the father of this world.

So, if you're wondering why I feel so secure, understand this...

He said it, and that settles it.

God is in control, I am on His side,

And that means all is well with my soul.

Every day is a blessing for GOD Is!

The joyful news is that not only can God give more than we ask for, He always does! This is particularly true with God's mercy.

A Personal Note

In the year 2002, my youngest daughter, Jerusha, age 22 at that time, was struggling with serious issues involving her physical health. A medical test revealed that one of her problems was a blockage in a blood vessel leading to her heart. My wife and I prayed much for her, and so did the fine church that I am privileged to pastor. Many others across the nation joined in offering prayers in her behalf.

Over a period of three to five weeks, she began to feel better. In September of that year, she had a series of three medical tests. Following these, the chief cardiologist in Mobile, Alabama examined her. The results of the first test had been shared with the doctor; the results of the other two tests were still pending.

Upon examining her and having reviewed the results of the first medical test, the cardiologist responded with utter amazement. He informed Jerusha that no blockage was visible and that he was quite sure it was gone. Then he noted to my daughter that her heart did not look like the same heart that he had previously examined. My daughter responded, "Well, I was prayed for."

The cardiologist was not ready to concede a miracle. His response was to the effect that he didn't know if it was the result of prayer or not; he just knew that it didn't look like the same heart. My feisty daughter responded, "It couldn't have been the medicine. I haven't been taking it. So, it must have been prayer."

When my wife and I received the news, we were thrilled but also astounded. We had been praying fervently for her healing. Transparently, though, we had never asked for or even thought of her being given a much-improved heart. We just wanted it to be okay. The Lord gave us more than we had requested. Such is His marvelous mercy!

Naaman

The story of Naaman is revealed in 2 Kings 5. He was the general over the Syrian Army. He was a great man and was both honorable and courageous. He had won many battles fought against other nations. However, in the course of his living, he was smitten with leprosy. He became a leper.

A little Hebrew slave girl witnessed to Naaman's wife. She told her of a man of God back in the land of Israel who could cure Naaman of this terrible plague. In desperation Naaman came to Israel with a single request—that he might be healed of his leprosy.

Once Naaman finally connected with the prophet of God, he was given instructions that were not to his liking. One of his servants politely, yet boldly, reasoned with Naaman and suggested that he try the proffered remedy. When Naaman came up out of the waters of the Jordan River, having dipped seven times, he discovered that he had been instantaneously healed. The Good Book declares, "and his flesh came again *like unto the flesh of a little child, and he was clean.*" [Emphasis added]

Don't overlook a great truth here. Not only was he healed, Naaman was given brand new skin! His skin was like that of a little child. The Lord gave Naaman more than he had asked for!

Zacharias

Consider the case of the priest named Zacharias. Luke 1 relates to us that Zacharias went into the Temple of the Lord to offer incense on the golden altar. He was faithfully executing his duty. The scriptures give enough insight for you and me to know that Zacharias took great pleasure in performing this custom.

The crowd praying outside the Temple marveled that Zacharias lingered so long inside. What they did not know and what Zacharias had not anticipated, was that Zacharias was being given more that day than just the privilege of burning incense.

An angel appeared to Zacharias. The angel named Gabriel was standing on the right side of the altar. The angel communicated with Zacharias and delivered a startling promise.

Zacharias and his wife were childless. Now Zacharias, an old man with an aged wife, was informed that he and his wife, Elisabeth, were going to produce a son. Not only that, but that his son would also become a great and powerful spiritual influence for the Lord. He would be used of God to lead a national revival in Israel. Many Israelites would be brought back to God through Zacharias' son's ministry.

Be sure to capture all the juice and flavor of this scriptural episode. Zacharias went into the Temple to offer incense and prayer. In addition to the joy of communion with God, here is what Zacharias received as a result of that one trip to God's House:

- A visitation by an angel;
- An answered prayer;

- A promise of a future blessing; namely, joy and gladness;
- A son; and,
- Confirmation that his promised son would be greatly used of God.

Zacharias finally came out of the Temple. When he arrived in the courtyard, he was unable to speak. This temporary impediment was because he had been filled with disbelief at the astounding gifts from God.

An observant reading of the passage in Luke 1 reveals that Zacharias had previously prayed for a son. It was a prayer that he had given up on and no longer prayed. How terrific that God remembered a prayer that Zacharias used to pray! The Lord answered a prayer that Zacharias had perhaps long ago shelved. The Lord not only answered the petition, but He certainly gave Zacharias much more than he had asked for.

Martha and Mary

Let's look at the story of the resurrection of Lazarus. It is recorded in John 11. We will review verses 1-5; 20-29; 32-35; 38-40; 43-44.

"Now a certain man was sick, named Lazarus, of Bethany, the town of Mary and her sister Martha.

(It was that Mary which anointed the Lord with ointment, and wiped his feet with her hair, whose brother Lazarus was sick.)

Therefore his sisters sent unto him, saying, Lord, behold, he whom thou lovest is sick.

When Jesus heard that, he said, This sickness is not unto death, but for the glory of God, that the Son of God might be glorified thereby.

Now Jesus loved Martha, and her sister, and Lazarus."

"Then Martha, as soon as she heard that Jesus was coming, went and met him: but Mary sat still in the house.

Then said Martha unto Jesus, Lord, if thou hadst been here, my brother had not died.

But I know, that even now, whatsoever thou wilt ask of God, God will give it thee.

Jesus saith unto her, Thy brother shall rise again.

Martha saith unto him, I know that he shall rise again in the resurrection at the last day.

Jesus said unto her, I am the resurrection, and the life: he that believeth in me, though he were dead, yet shall he live:

And whosoever liveth and believeth in me shall never die. Believest thou this?

She saith unto him, Yea, Lord: I believe that thou art the Christ, the Son of God, which should come into the world.

And when she had so said, she went her way, and called Mary her sister secretly, saying, The Master is come, and calleth for thee.

As soon as she heard that, she arose quickly, and came unto him."

"Then when Mary was come where Jesus was, and saw him, she fell down at his feet, saying unto him, Lord, if thou hadst been here, my brother had not died.

When Jesus therefore saw her weeping, and the Jews also weeping which came with her, he groaned in the spirit, and was troubled,

And said, Where have ye laid him? They said unto him, Lord, come and see.

Jesus wept."

"Jesus therefore again groaning in himself cometh to the grave. It was a cave, and a stone lay upon it.

Jesus said, Take ye away the stone. Martha, the sister of him that was dead, saith unto him, Lord, by this time he stinketh: for he hath been dead four days.

Jesus saith unto her, Said I not unto thee, that, if thou wouldest believe, thou shouldest see the glory of God?"

"And when he thus had spoken, he cried with a loud voice, Lazarus, come forth.

And he that was dead came forth, bound hand and foot with graveclothes: and his face was bound about with a napkin. Jesus saith unto them, Loose him, and let him go."

It must be noted that, in verse 3, Martha and Mary simply notified Jesus that Lazarus was gravely ill. We could speculate as to the reasons why, but the evidence is that there was no urgent appeal attached to this notice. Specifically, they did not ask for Jesus to come and heal their brother.

When the Lord did arrive at Bethany, Lazarus had been dead for four days. Both Martha and Mary made it clear to Jesus that they truly believed that if Jesus had been present with them before Lazarus succumbed, the Lord would have prevented his death. However, even these bold expressions of faith had no present petition attached to them.

Martha did say in verse 22 that she believed that, even at the present moment, whatever Jesus asked for in prayer would be granted by God. Still she did not make any appeal for prayer to Jesus. There was no request for intervention. As a matter of fact, when Jesus suggested the resurrection of Lazarus, she deflected the idea by noting that the proper timing for such an event was at the end of the age. Simply put, she just couldn't imagine such a momentous event happening in the present moment.

Case in point: when Jesus ordered the stone removed from the grave's mouth and it became apparent that He was preparing to take some action, Martha insinuated that it was not a good option to attempt such a thing. She noted that there were serious side effects that would be encountered in such an operation; namely, decay and foul odor. It was a classic display of dense reasoning and shallow faith. He that can overpower the grave can most certainly remove decay and cleanse the person and the atmosphere of its stench.

Lazarus was called out of the burial cave. He was assisted in shedding the grave clothes. He hugged his sisters, and they joyfully returned home together. They had a lot to talk about that evening. Jesus had given Martha and Mary not only more than they had asked for but also more than they dreamed was even a possibility. He delights in blessing folks that way.

The Women at the Tomb

Mary Magdalene, Mary the mother of James, Salome, and perhaps some other women journeyed to the sepulcher to see the place of Jesus' burial and to anoint His body. The overriding concern on their minds as they traveled towards the tomb was finding someone to roll away the mammoth stone from the grave's mouth.

At the first crack of dawn, they approached the sepulcher. To their surprise, the stone was already rolled aside. As they entered the opening of the tomb, an angel greeted them. The heavenly visitor announced to them that Jesus was risen and very much alive. The ladies hurriedly left the empty grave, shaken by what they had just seen and heard. They certainly got more that morning than they had expected.

After the other women left the tomb area, Mary Magdalene lingered in the surrounding garden. It was to her that Jesus first appeared after His resurrection. She never asked for that and never even conceived of it happening. Yet, on that first Easter morning, she got a whole lot more than anything she had asked for or even thought. It is a specialty of Jesus to delight people in this fashion.

God's Response to Backsliders

It is necessary to take a few moments to evaluate God's response to backsliders. Luke 15 tells the story of the prodigal son. It is the story of a backslider.

Verse 13 says that the young man went into "a *far* country." There he "*wasted* his substance with riotous living." Eventually, he "spent *all*" (verse 14). [Emphasis added]

Fortunately, there came a day when "he came to himself" (verse 17). It was a moment of spiritual sanity. He determined to return to his father's house and began the long journey home. He prepared his appeal for mercy to his father. It was an appeal straight from the heart. His plea would be, "Father, I have sinned against heaven, and before thee, and am no more worthy to be called thy son: make me as one of thy hired servants." In other words, "Just let me be an employee. I ask for nothing more."

As the prodigal was approaching the home place, though yet a great way off, the father recognized his familiar form. Observe the immediate response of the father upon seeing his wayward son:

- He had *compassion* on him;
- He ran to the son;
- He *fell* on his neck; and,
- He kissed him.

This was already much more than the prodigal thought he deserved or even hoped to receive. However, the father was not through giving. The father told his servants to give the son these additional amenities:

- The best robe;
- A ring for his hand;
- Shoes for his bare feet;
- The fatted calf (such were slaughtered for special occasions), to feed him; and,
- A celebration to welcome the son home.

Surrounded by merriment, music, and dancing, one has to believe that the repentant prodigal found it all hard to believe and could scarce contain his joy. The father had given him so much more than he had requested.

The father in this parable is representative of God Almighty. This story clearly reveals God's willingness to receive back those who have left His house and family. He will not only welcome backsliders into His arms again, He will shock and surprise them with the abundance of His showered

THE LORD WILL GIVE RECOVERED PRODIGALS MORE THAN THEY EVER IMAGINED.

gifts. The Lord will give recovered prodigals more than they ever imagined. You have to understand—this is just the Father's *modus operandi* or His standard operating procedure.

The Lord Gives More than We Request

God's Response to Sinners

Luke 23 records Christ's crucifixion. The account includes the dialogue between Jesus and a repentant thief who was being executed simultaneously on a nearby cross. The humbled and praying thief asked a sincere request of Jesus in verse 42, "Lord, remember me when thou comest into thy kingdom." It was a concise, but nonetheless revelatory, plea.

Careful analysis of the dialogue reveals that Jesus did not give the thief that for which he asked. He gave him more—much more!

If Jesus had precisely answered the prayer of this repentant thief, it would have been 2,000 years or more before this questing man received his desired fulfillment. However, Jesus gave the converted thief way more than that for which he had asked. In effect, Jesus responded, "I am not going to wait 2,000 years to include you—*today* you will be with me in paradise."

In retrospect, the humbled and dying man requested only to be remembered by Christ at some future time. Instead, Jesus welcomed him that very day into paradise. That repentant soul went into eternity knowing that the Lord had given him more than he had requested. What a world-class demonstration of God's marvelous mercy!

It is this same marvelous mercy that is the underpinning of our own personal hope for eternal life. We should obey God's Word and seek daily to please Him. However, ultimately, there is no hope of any of us being saved apart from God's mercy.

The New Testament writer, Jude, identifies what the present focus of believers should be in verses 20-21. I quote the Moffatt version and add one last emphasis.

"But do you, beloved, build up yourselves on your most holy faith and pray in the holy Spirit,

so keeping yourselves within the love of God and **waiting for the mercy of our Lord Jesus Christ that ends in life eternal**."

Mercy...that results in life eternal!

That is marvelous mercy indeed!

Ministry Contact
Information

To schedule the author for speaking engagements, you may contact him as follows:

ROBERT E. HENSON
P. O. Box 7008

Flint, MI 48507

Phone: 810-743-1710

Fax: 810-743-9851

*Other Books
By*

ROBERT E. HENSON

- **EFFECTIVE ALTAR MINISTRY**
  How to pray with persons who are reaching out to God

- **THE SILHOUETTE OF MAJESTY**
  Insights into the Person and work of the Lord Jesus Christ

- **PRAYER FORCE ONE**
  Helpful concepts on how to build an effective personal prayer life

- **LIVING A BALANCED LIFE...**
  IN AN UNBALANCED WORLD
  Inspiration and instruction for victorious Christian living

To purchase any of these books, contact him as follows:

ROBERT E. HENSON

P. O. Box 7008

Flint, MI 48507

Phone: 810-743-1710
Fax: 810-743-9851